To the Far Side of Hell

The Battle for Peleliu, 1944

Dedication

For Ollie Sweetland

TO THE FAR SIDE OF HELL

The Battle for Peleliu, 1944

Derrick Wright

The Crowood Press

First published in 2002 by
The Crowood Press Ltd
Ramsbury, Marlborough
Wiltshire SN8 2HR

Edited by Martin Windrow

British Library Cataloguing-in-Publication Data
A catalogue record for this book is available from the British Library.

ISBN 1 86126 544 1

Typeset by Phoenix Typesetting
Burley-in-Wharfedale, West Yorkshire

Printed and bound in Great Britain by The Cromwell Press, Trowbridge

Contents

Acknowledgements

As with my previous books on the Pacific conflict, I have received generous and unreserved help from veterans of the battle, to whom I extend my heartfelt thanks. Quoted material has not been altered beyond amendments to standardise punctuation. I would particularly like to thank the following:

The late Tom Lea, the US Army Center for Military History and the Stillpoint Press, Dallas, Texas, for permission to reproduce some of Tom Lea's outstanding paintings and drawings (the chapter title sketches are the originals made by Lea on Peleliu).

For permission to quote from their books and papers on the battle: Bob Boardman, Jim Johnston and Larry L.Woodward.

For information about their parts in the battle of Peleliu:

John C.Brewer, Thomas G.Climie, Gen. Ray Davis MOH, the late Brooking Rouse Gex, Col. Larry A.Greene, Fred E.Harris, Jeb Lord, Sterling G.Mace, James W.Moll, Jack McCombs, Edward Newell, Charles H.Owen, Preston S.Parrish, Robert F.Singer, Robert D.Sohrt, Oliver L.Sweetland, R.Bruce Watkins and Lawrence Wilkinson.

The wartime photographs of the battle are reproduced courtesy of the National Archives, Washington DC, the US Marine Corps, the US Navy and the US Air Force. Contemporary photographs of Peleliu are by courtesy of David M.Green and Eric Mailander. The maps are by the author unless otherwise individually credited.

Preface

The battle for Peleliu, fought by a joint force from the 1st Division of the United States Marine Corps and the US Army's 81st Division in September 1944, is one of the least-known battles not only of the Pacific campaign, but of the entire Second World War. Due to limited reporting, the obscurity of the location, and the perceived view that events in Europe were more newsworthy, the battle went almost unnoticed by the American public of the time.

At a Marine Corps reunion in 1998 I asked a veteran of Iwo Jima if he knew anything about Peleliu. 'Vaguely', he replied; and that pretty well sums up present day knowledge of one of the war's grimmest battles – something vaguely remembered from late 1944, and referred to even now by the Marine Corps as the 'forgotten battle'. (Indeed, when President Harry Truman came to place the Medal of Honor around the neck of one of the heroes of the battle, he could not pronounce its name.)

Yet Peleliu was one of the bloodiest battles of the whole Pacific campaign – the bloodiest, according to many 1st Division veterans who had earlier served at Guadalcanal and Cape Gloucester, and who after Peleliu were to endure the hell of Okinawa. The greatest tragedy of all is that, viewed in retrospect, the battle need never have been fought at all.

* * *

By the summer of 1944 the Japanese victories at Pearl Harbor, in the Philippines, at Hong Kong, Singapore and in the Dutch East Indies – the milestones of their lightning advance across the Pacific in December 1941 and early 1942 – were a fading memory. The American war machine had moved into top gear; men, guns, tanks, ships, aircraft and supplies were pouring across the Atlantic and Pacific Oceans in awesome quantities, and Admiral Yamamoto's prediction after Pearl Harbor that 'we have wakened a sleeping giant' was proving to be tragically prophetic for the Japanese.

On the South-East Asian mainland British and Commonwealth troops of the 14th Army had just smashed Japan's last offensive towards the borders of India at Kohima and Imphal, and within weeks would begin driving the enemy relentlessly east and south through the jungles of Burma. Meanwhile, two giant claws were already tearing at the hopelessly over-extended perimeter held by the Imperial Army and Navy in the Pacific.

General Douglas MacArthur, as Supreme Allied Commander South-West Pacific in command of joint American and Australian forces, was driving through New Guinea and Indonesia towards the Philippines, from where he had been ignominiously evacuated in March 1942. He had made his famous pledge – 'I shall return' – as he left the besieged island of Corregidor, and a return in triumph was now his overriding ambition. In a series of brilliantly executed amphibious leaps, he had taken Manus, Los Negros and Biak, and was poised to attack Morotai, from where he could mount an assault on the island of Mindanao, the largest of the southern Philippine Islands.

In the Central Pacific, Adm. Chester Nimitz, Commander-in-Chief Pacific Fleet (CINCPAC), was leading five Marine divisions and the world's largest navy in an 'island-hopping' campaign that would bring his Marines to the very doorstep of the Japanese mainland. Starting at the tiny atoll of Tarawa in the Gilbert Islands in November 1943, the Marines had undergone a baptism of fire and blood which taught them costly lessons in the art of mounting amphibious attacks against heavily defended islands. From Tarawa the juggernaut had moved on to the Marshall Islands; and then to Guam, Saipan and Tinian in the Marianas, where huge airfields were being constructed for the new Boeing B-29 Superfortress long range bombers to launch their fire-raising attacks on the Japanese home islands.

By early 1944, influential personalities within the Army and Navy were at loggerheads as to which was the better strategy. It seemed to many that a choice would have to be made between them at some point, in order to concentrate for the final effort: America's resources of manpower and matériel were vast, but not limitless. Admiral Ernest J.King, Chief of Naval Operations, pressed for Nimitz's option of a direct assault on the Japanese mainland spearheaded by his Marines, while the Army faction favoured MacArthur's preferred route via the Philippines and Formosa (now Taiwan). In a bid to resolve the situation, President Franklin D.Roosevelt decided to sail to Hawaii and meet his two supreme commanders to hear their arguments at first hand.

At the meeting in July 1944, the President opened the agenda with the question, 'Where do we go from here?', and sat back to absorb the reactions of his commanders. MacArthur gave a long and well-prepared presentation of his strategy, ending with his trump card: the American promise to the people of the Philippines that they would eventually return to drive the Japanese out. The President listened in silence, while sizing up the general; it was well known that there was little love lost between the two. MacArthur, backed by a powerful lobby of Republican newspaper tycoons including William Randolph Hearst and Robert MacCormick, had his eyes firmly set on the presidency of the United States after Roosevelt's unprecedented fourth term of office came to an end. Roosevelt had a hearty dislike of the arrogant general, but did not undervalue his military talents.

One of the most complex and controversial commanders of the war, MacArthur was acknowledged as a brilliant leader who had an almost instinctive ability to strike the enemy where and when it would cause the most damage. A classic example of the old fashioned 'army brat', MacArthur was the son of a Civil War hero who had won the Medal of Honor at Missionary Ridge and later served as military governor of the Philippines. Douglas MacArthur had graduated at the top of his West Point class in 1903, and had demonstrated a driving ambition throughout his career; twice wounded in the First World War, he had risen to command a division in 1918. His inter-war career had included several postings to the Philippines, whose fledgling army he had commanded in the 1930s. He was renowned for his personal bravery in action, often walking to the front line and beyond to view the enemy positions; the disparaging nickname 'Dug-out Doug' bestowed on him by some of his beleaguered troops in spring 1942 was hardly just.

As a man, his vanity was his principal shortcoming. It is difficult to find a photograph of him in which he is not skilfully posing for the camera, and his eccentricities of dress – the sunglasses, the artfully crumpled cap of a Filipino field-marshal, the folksy corncob pipe – were all part of what today would be seen as 'image-making'.

By complete contrast, Chester Nimitz, born at Fredericksburg in Texas of German stock, was an introverted, studious and formal man whose brilliant campaigns had earned him the high regard of the Chiefs of Staff after he had been rushed to Hawaii in 1941 to succeed Adm. Kimmel following the Pearl Harbor disaster. Nimitz had gathered around him an outstanding team of Navy and Marine officers. Among them were Adm. Raymond Spruance, an even more self-contained personality than Nimitz, who was behind the planning of all the amphibious operations from Tarawa to Iwo Jima; and Adm. William 'Bull' Halsey, the flamboyant task force and fleet commander. These two officers jointly held command of the main Navy fighting force in the Central Pacific, alternating in seagoing command and periods of preparatory staff work; confusingly, when Spruance flew his flag at sea it was designated the 5th Fleet, and when Halsey took over, the 3rd Fleet, with component task forces changing their designations accordingly (e.g. from TF58 to TF38). Vice Admiral Marc 'Oklahoma Pete' Mitscher was a gifted commander of aircraft carrier task forces; and Vice Admiral Richmond Kelly Turner knew more about putting troops ashore than any other officer in the Navy. Nimitz's aggressive Marine commander was Lieutenant-General Holland M.Smith – a volatile officer universally known to his men as 'Howlin' Mad' – whose difficult personality was off-set by his unique expertise in amphibious operations.

At the Hawaii conference Nimitz, in his characteristically dry and well-organised manner, made his proposals to Roosevelt for a continuation of his present policy: making landings on vital islands, by-passing those that had no strategic value or were geographically unsuitable for amphibious operations, 'island-hopping' ever nearer to Japan while his carrier task forces hounded the remains of the Imperial Japanese Navy to the very shores of the homeland.

The President listened to the arguments; studied the maps; and told his commanders that he would make his decisions known on the following day. The conference had been long and tiring for the ailing President, and he needed time to mull over the masses of information that he had been given. When they came, his decisions were in fact ambivalent. MacArthur had made a good impression, and was given the go-ahead to liberate the Philippines from the south using all available Army units then in the Pacific; Nimitz would give full naval and air support from his carrier forces.

Three months before the meeting, Nimitz had sent an order to the commanding general of the 1st Marine Division to invade Peleliu in the Palau Islands 'no later than 15 September'; and nothing was said at the Hawaii conference to cause him to change that order. Thus Operation Stalemate, which included the invasion of Peleliu and the neighbouring island of Angaur, was put into motion. A combination of poor planning, hesitant leadership, and a dramatic change in the Japanese defence strategy was to turn what had been expected to be a short, fierce operation into a bloody two-and-a-half-month nightmare.

CHAPTER 1

Plans and Planners

The Quadrant Conference, held in Quebec in August 1943 between President Roosevelt, British Prime Minister Winston Churchill and the Allied Chiefs of Staff, had been called to lay down the long-term strategy for the future conduct of the war. The overriding concern was the proposed invasion of Europe (Operation Overlord), but the Pacific campaign was also high on the agenda. There was overwhelming support for MacArthur's proposed invasion of the Philippines; but with the huge build-up of US naval strength and the predicted expansion of the Marine Corps to a massive 175,000 men by early 1944, it was agreed that Adm. Nimitz should be given a free hand to exploit the ever-changing military and naval situation in the Central Pacific.

A high priority for Nimitz was the invasion of the Mariana Islands – specifically Guam, Saipan and Tinian – where the US Army Air Force were anxious to locate airfields from which their B-29 Superfortress bombers could mount attacks on the Japanese mainland. But before such an invasion could be contemplated, the Caroline Islands had to be dealt with. Stretching from Kusai, adjacent to the Marshalls in the east, to the Palaus in the west, the Carolines encompass over 550 small islands and atolls a few hundred miles north of the equator.

* * *

Japan had supported the Allies during the First World War, and part of her booty had been former German island colonies in the Pacific – the Palaus, Carolines and Marianas. The Japanese had seen their strategic importance long before the attack on Pearl Harbor, and had established three major strongholds in the Carolines – Truk, Yap and Ulithi. When Nimitz and his team in Hawaii had initially planned the invasion of the Palaus it was to facilitate attacks on these three vital locations. However, with MacArthur's invasion of the southern Philippines now high on the agenda, the neutralisation of the Palaus, and particularly the island of Peleliu with its large airfield, was vital to protect MacArthur's eastern flank.

When they occupied the Palaus the Japanese had set up a civil and military administration at Koror, located between the large northern island of Babelthuap and Urukthapel to the south (see Map 1, page 15). A considerable amount of development had been undertaken; the docks and harbours had been vastly improved, and paved roads with electric lighting, factories and a hospital were provided. Along with the improvements came several thousand Japanese immigrants, anxious to exploit the natural resources of the islands. Phosphate was the only mineral of any value and refineries were built on Peleliu and the neighbouring island of Angaur, although these had been abandoned by 1944. The major military constructions of this period were a large 'A'-type airfield built on the flat southern end of Peleliu,

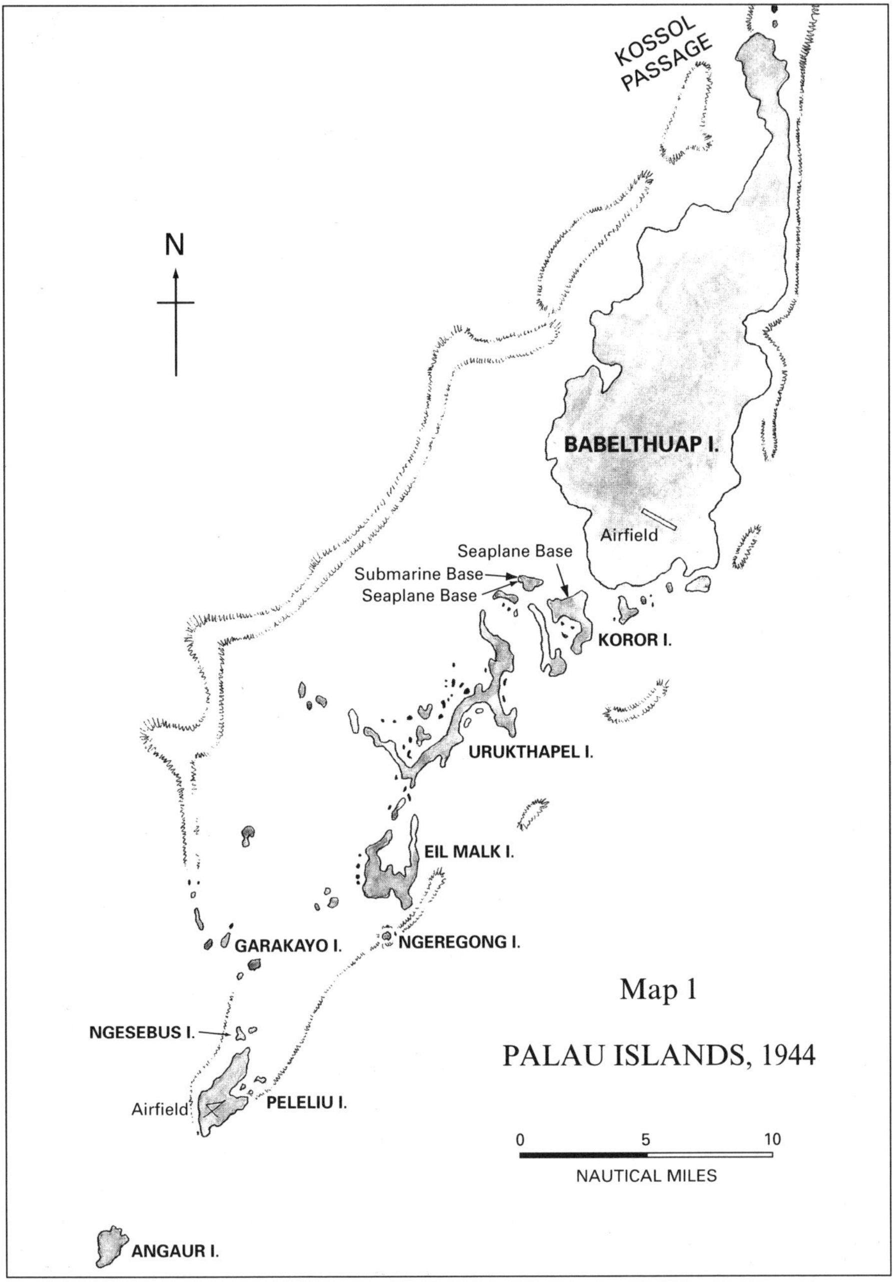
N
KOSSOL PASSAGE
BABELTHUAP I.
Airfield
Seaplane Base
Submarine Base
Seaplane Base
KOROR I.
URUKTHAPEL I.
EIL MALK I.
GARAKAYO I.
NGEREGONG I.
NGESEBUS I.
Airfield
PELELIU I.
ANGAUR I.
Map 1
PALAU ISLANDS, 1944
0
5
10
NAUTICAL MILES

completed in 1938, and a smaller airfield on Babelthuap. A seaplane base was also constructed on the island of Arekebesan to the west of Koror.

When the Japanese attacked the Philippines in December 1941 an Imperial Navy carrier task force from Peleliu joined with bomber squadrons based on Formosa to neutralise the American airfields, and within days all US airpower on the islands had been destroyed. The Palaus were also an important staging post for troops invading the Philippines, and later New Guinea and the Solomon Islands. As the war turned against the Japanese in late 1943, the Carolines became part of the Empire's vital second line of defence.

In the second week of February 1944, Task Force 58, a huge armada of carriers, battleships, cruisers and destroyers under the command of Adm. Mitscher, struck the Japanese naval base of Truk in the central Caroline Islands. Its vast lagoon provided a superb natural anchorage, and the Japanese had developed Truk into a formidable bastion with batteries of heavy naval guns, airfields housing over 400 aircraft, and an estimated garrison of 3,500 troops. Admiral Nimitz and his planners had so far been reluctant to mount an invasion of this 'Gibraltar of the Pacific'; the details of Truk's defences could only be guessed at, but they were clearly formidable. Indeed, the original intention of starting the American 'island-hopping' offensive in the Marshall Islands had been modified in favour of the more southerly Gilberts for fear of a major retaliation by Imperial Navy forces based at Truk.

Mitscher's carrier air attacks of February 1944 lasted for two days, as wave upon wave of torpedo- and dive-bombers, supported by flotillas of fighters, blasted the enemy installations. The Japanese had probably had warning of the approaching armada, since they had hastily evacuated most of their heavy warships. Nevertheless, 'Oklahoma Pete's' pilots sank two cruisers, four destroyers, two submarines and over 200,000 tons of cargo shipping; 250 enemy aircraft were destroyed, and heavy damage was inflicted on airfields and ground installations. So successful was the attack that a jubilant Nimitz decided to delete Truk from his list of targets for invasion, and the island was not occupied by the Americans until after the Japanese surrender in 1945.

The effective loss of Truk obliged the Japanese to concentrate their next line of defence on the Palau Islands. The naval presence was to be boosted; and Adm. Koga, the successor as C-in-C Japanese Combined Fleet to the brilliant Adm. Yamamoto – who had been killed over Bougainville in April 1943 when his plane was shot down by American fighters – decided temporarily to set up his headquarters on Koror. Koga left Japan in the super-battleship *Musashi* (at 72,000 tons, one of the two largest battleships ever built); but his arrival coincided with attacks on the Palaus by

Mitscher's task force on 30–31 March, and he spent two days anchored offshore monitoring reports of the devastation being inflicted. (At one stage the *Musashi* was buzzed by US fighters, but inexplicably no attack was mounted.) Mitscher's pilots struck Koror, Babelthuap and Peleliu; the airfield on Babelthuap was virtually destroyed, Peleliu's airfield received heavy damage to the runways and surrounding installations, and many Japanese aircraft were destroyed. The smaller fighter strip under construction on the island of Ngesebus off the northern tip of Peleliu was also damaged. In addition, virtually all the Japanese ships in the Palaus were sunk or crippled. Admiral Nimitz was overjoyed with the results of the operation: 'The Western Carolines are at least temporarily neutralized, MacArthur's right flank is safe'. This statement casts a puzzling light on his decision to go ahead with landings on Peleliu only months later.

In the battle of the Philippine Sea in June 1944, US submarines and Adm. Mitscher's carrier force stripped the Imperial Navy of three fleet carriers, 480 aircraft and hundreds of their remaining naval pilots in what became known as 'the Great Marianas Turkey Shoot'. Thereafter the US task forces were able to roam almost at will in the Central Pacific.

General MacArthur was adamant that both his western and eastern flanks should be secure before he embarked on his invasion of the Philippines in mid-November. He would himself oversee the capture of Morotai Island in the Molucca Sea using 28,000 US Army troops, while the Palaus were to be the responsibility of Adm. Nimitz. The airfield on Peleliu, only 500 miles from the Philippines, was the obvious threat; but after Mitscher's devastating attacks in March, and the crushing defeat of the Japanese Navy in the Philippine Sea in June, it is difficult to understand why Peleliu was still considered so important in September. Photo reconnaissance revealed that the airfield was still in a sorry state, with serious damage to the installations unrepaired and large numbers of wrecked aircraft littering the area. Its value was in any case academic, since the Japanese did not have sufficient airpower anywhere in the western Carolines to threaten an American invasion of the Philippines; and with a complete absence of Japanese naval forces in the area, the US Navy task forces were in a position to totally isolate the Palaus.

This leads us to the most important question about the whole operation: why was the Peleliu invasion plan implemented? To seek an answer it is necessary to examine the complex strategic situation at that crucial period of the Pacific War.

In a directive issued in March 1944, Adm. Nimitz had been instructed by the Joint Chiefs of Staff to occupy the Marianas–Palaus line; a chain of command was established under the codename Stalemate, with the proposed invasion of the Palaus set for September.

A warning order was issued at the end of May, envisaging a very ambitious operation to occupy the whole of the Palau Islands: the 1st Division of the Marine Corps and the 81st Division of the US Army were to take Peleliu and the adjacent island of Angaur, while the Army's 7th and 77th Divisions were assigned the larger island of Babelthuap, and the 27th Division was to be held in reserve.

The invasion of the Marianas Islands in June and July, to secure airfields for the USAAF's Superfortresses, caused Nimitz to drastically modify Stalemate. The Army's 77th Division was diverted to Guam, and the 27th Division, the proposed reserves, went to Saipan. In the Palaus, the Japanese had concentrated the bulk of their Army units in the north with Koror as the military headquarters; an attack in this sector, particularly with inexperienced Army troops, would involve considerable risks. The planners were also becoming concerned about the geography of Babelthuap; reconnaissance flights over the island revealed it to be a mass of dense jungle, a terrain in which the Army could become bogged down for months. Consequently the operation plan was modified, and a second order, codenamed Stalemate 2, was issued. Babelthuap was omitted from Stalemate 2, and Yap and the atoll of Ulithi in the Carolines were substituted. The operation was now divided into two sections. The Eastern Attack Force, comprising the Army's 7th and 96th Divisions, would occupy Yap and Ulithi; the Western Force, which would remain the 1st Marine Division and the Army's 81st, would take Peleliu and Angaur.

* * *

In early September 1944, Adm. Halsey, commander of the 3rd Fleet, arrived in the Philippine Sea and rendezvoused with Mitscher's Task Force 38 to cover both Stalemate 2 operations. In conversations with Mitscher he was amazed to discover that there had been virtually no opposition to a series of carrier-based air attacks throughout the island of Mindanao in the southern Philippines – MacArthur's planned first target for the liberation. Halsey at once ordered more flights, and between 12 and 13 September over 2,400 sorties were carried out; once again, the Japanese were conspicuous by their absence. Further evidence was forthcoming from a rescued US Navy pilot who had been forced to land in the Philippines: he reported that the natives who had helped him were adamant that there were few Japanese on Mindanao, or on Leyte to the north.

Halsey immediately contacted Nimitz, MacArthur and King, informing them of the light opposition in the area, and expressing the belief that the Palaus operation was not now necessary to support the Philippines invasion. It was 12 September when Nimitz received the message from Halsey – just three days before the Peleliu invasion was due to commence.

The 1st Marine Division were already en route from Pavuvu in the Russell Islands where they had been assembling and training. There followed a flurry of message traffic between the various commanders involved in Stalemate 2 and the Joint Chiefs of Staff in Washington. The outcome of these discussions was confirmation that MacArthur would now abandon his proposed invasion of Mindanao and go straight for Leyte. The final decision about Peleliu remained with Nimitz.

Why then did Nimitz decide to continue with the attack on Peleliu? We may look for clarification in messages exchanged during September between Nimitz and Halsey. In one the CINCPAC expressed the view that the seizure of Peleliu, Angaur and Ulithi was necessary not only to secure MacArthur's flank as originally planned, but to 'facilitate advances into the Formosa–Luzon–China coast area and operations against objectives to the northward'. In a message to Adm. King in Washington he expressed the view that the occupation of the Palaus and Ulithi was 'essential', and that it was not feasible to alter the plans as rapidly as Halsey had suggested.

Over the years a plethora of theories have been put forward to try to explain Nimitz's motivation for pressing on with the Peleliu invasion. It has been suggested that he became overconfident after the rapid conquest of the Marshall Islands and parts of the Marianas (Tinian took only nine days); or that he was influenced by the predictions of the commander of the 1st Marine Division, Gen. Rupertus, who boasted that Peleliu would only take three days to capture. Another theory is that with Rupertus' division already at sea, it was too late to cancel such a massive undertaking.

Chester Nimitz was one of the finest commanders of the war, a thoughtful man who was acutely aware that his decisions could mean life or death to thousands of his men, and who took the burden of this knowledge very much to heart. The suggestion that he would implement an operation of this size through sheer reluctance to change his plans (at a time when a far more fundamental change had just been made to MacArthur's plans), or that he could be influenced by the overconfident predictions of one of his divisional commanders, is beyond belief. Whatever his reasons – which must remain among the unsolved mysteries of the war – we may be sure that they were based on a genuine belief that the invasion was a necessary step in the overall plan for the Pacific campaign as it appeared to him at that time.

* * *

The command structure for the operation was a complex one, as was true of most of the Pacific invasions, but a brief review is necessary if we are to understand the progress of the battle.

Overall command of the ground forces was held by Maj. Gen. Julian

C.Smith USMC as Commander, Expeditionary Troops, 3rd Fleet. It was Smith who had overseen the Marine Corps' first full-scale amphibious landing operation at Tarawa the previous November as commander of the 2nd Marine Division. The Western Attack Force (Southern Palaus) was the responsibility of III Amphibious Corps under Maj.Gen. Roy S.Geiger USMC; a Marine aviator, Geiger was the former chief of the 'Cactus Air Force', the original air wing on Guadalcanal. Geiger's major components were the 1st Marine Division and the Army's 81st Division. The commander of the 1st Marine Division was Maj.Gen. William H.Rupertus, the former divisional second-in-command. The 81st Division was led by Maj.Gen. Paul J.Mueller, US Army, an able veteran of the First World War.

The 1st Marine Division was essentially a 'triangular' organisation, whose fighting core was three regiments of Marine infantry, each of three battalions. (The USMC habitually refer to their numbered regiments simply as e.g. 1st Marines, 7th Marines, etc.; but to avoid confusion between regiments and other units and formations, they will sometimes be referred to specifically as 'regiments' in this text.)

The 1st Regiment's commander was Colonel Lewis B.Puller. Already an admired figure in the Corps, 'Chesty' Puller would survive to become a living legend. He was a veteran of the 'Banana Wars' fought against guerrilla bandits in the jungles of Haiti and Nicaragua in the 1920s and 1930s; he had distinguished himself as a battalion commander in the 7th Marines on Guadalcanal; he would distinguish himself once more on Peleliu, and years later would earn still wider fame during the Korean War.

The 5th Marines were led by Col. Harold D.Harris, the youngest of the three regimental commanders and regarded as something of an intellectual – he had attended the Ecole Superieure de Guerre in Paris in 1938/39. 'Bucky' Harris had assumed command only weeks before the Peleliu operation, but his performance during the battle was to prove equal to that of any of his brother officers.

The 7th Marines were commanded by Col. Herman H.Hanneken, another 'Banana Wars' veteran and a holder of the Medal of Honor, America's supreme decoration for valour. Hanneken was a rather stoic and forbidding character who had earned the nickname 'Hard Head', perhaps a legacy of his German ancestry.

Around this backbone of infantry, the Marine force included a wide variety of support and service units, both integral to the 1st Division and attached from the assets of the higher commands. The total numbers looked impressive: Marines 26,417 all ranks, including attached units; Army, 21,108 – a grand total of 47,525 men. However, these figures are deceptive.

The capture of Angaur would occupy two Regimental Combat Teams (RCTs) of the 81st Division, and Adm. Nimitz had earmarked its third RCT to capture Ulithi; this meant that there were virtually no reserves during the first phase of the Peleliu invasion. Moreover, although the Marine strength stood at more than 26,000, only around 10,000 of these were infantrymen. The realistic ratio of assault troops to defenders was little better than one-to-one – frighteningly low, given the lessons of previous opposed landings.

On the plus side, the naval support for the operation could only be described as massive. Vice-Admiral Wilkinson's Task Force 31 was responsible for getting the troops ashore, while a Fire Support Group of Task Force 34 under Rear Adm. Jesse Oldendorf was to soften up the island. The battleships USS *Maryland, Idaho, Mississippi* and *Pennsylvania,* together with the heavy cruisers *Louisville, Portland* and *Indianapolis* and the light cruiser *Honolulu,* plus nine destroyers, could deliver a punch that was expected to eliminate all enemy opposition. For the Angaur phase of the attack one battleship, the *Tennessee,* and one heavy cruiser, the *Minneapolis*, accompanied by the light cruisers *Denver, Cleveland* and *Columbus*, were to provide support for the Army landings. Air cover would be provided by hundreds of planes from eight carriers, bombing and strafing at will – Japanese air cover was to be non-existent.

* * *

It was at this stage of the war that the Japanese made a radical change to their defensive strategy. Up to 1944 the defence of the islands and atolls of the Central Pacific had been the responsibility of the Special Landing Forces of the Imperial Navy, but after the shattering defeat in the battle of the Philippine Sea it fell to the Imperial Army to secure these areas.

One of the Army's most distinguished formations was the 14th (Utsunomiya) Division. Originally formed in 1905, it had led the attack during the capture of Port Arthur in the Russo-Japanese War of that year. During the operations in China in the 1930s it had served with 4th Army of the Kwangtung (Area) Army in Manchuria. Its infantry group comprised the 2nd (Mito), 15th (Maebashi) and 59th (Utsunomiya) Infantry Regiments. In early 1944, the 14th was stationed at Tsitsihar in Manchuria; but in February the division was alerted to transfer to the Palaus. The divisional commander, Lt.Gen. Sadae Inoue, was summoned to Tokyo by the Prime Minister and War Minister, Gen. Tojo, who left him in no doubt that his mission was to hold the islands for as long as possible, and to kill as many Americans as possible – there were not expected to be any Japanese survivors. Within weeks, troop transports were on their way; the division was transported by a long and circuitous route to avoid the American submarines which were then achieving very high 'kill' rates in the Pacific, but by the end of April 1944 they were in place.

General Inoue's first task was to tour the islands by road and air to assess the situation. He quickly realised that the large northern island of Babelthuap was geographically unsuitable for defence; and that Koror would be of little value to the enemy.

It was clear that Peleliu and Angaur were the Americans' targets; the airfield on Peleliu was the jackpot, and it would not be feasible to hold Peleliu without securing Angaur too. For the defence of Peleliu, Gen. Inoue deployed the 3,280-strong 2nd Infantry Regiment under its commander Col. Kunio Nakagawa, a much-decorated veteran of the China wars and an officer who had been singled out for senior promotion. A number of other units were attached to Nakagawa's command, principally some 1,700 extra infantry – one battalion from the division's 15th Infantry Regiment and another from the 53rd Independent Infantry Brigade. For the defence of Angaur the general despatched two battalions of the 14th Division's 59th Infantry Regiment, numbering 1,500 men, under Maj. Ushio Goto. Other Japanese on the islands included some 1,000 Navy combat troops, 2,000 labourers of Navy construction units, and perhaps 2,000 Naval Air Force personnel.

Colonel Nakagawa's first obstacle was another Japanese officer. The Imperial Navy still had a senior ranking officer in charge of Peleliu, an admiral, and the inter-service rivalries that pervaded the Japanese forces throughout the war were undiminished. The admiral flatly refused to co-operate with a lower ranking Army officer. General Inoue solved the problem by appointing Maj.Gen. Kenijiro Murai, senior in rank to the admiral, as overall commander of Peleliu. General Murai and Col. Nakagawa got on well together, and would fight as equals when the invasion came in September.

During the early preparations to defend Japanese-held islands against American amphibious landings, the overriding concern had been to halt the enemy at the water's edge; but it had become increasingly obvious that this tactic was not working. At Tarawa the Imperial Navy garrison had constructed a strong perimeter defence all round the island of Betio, but had wrongly anticipated the site of the USMC landings, thus wasting the potential of many of their excellently protected and camouflaged emplacements. Although a serious American misjudgement of the depth of water over the reefs had condemned many of the Marines of the 2nd Division to wading waist-deep towards the shore in the face of murderous artillery and small arms fire, the Americans still made significant gains, and as reinforcements came ashore they beat the Japanese back from their tough but thin defensive shell. With no defence in depth, once the beaches were secured the Japanese opposition generally crumbled, ending in frenzied *banzai* attacks which inevitably achieved nothing but wholesale sacrifice. Things were to be different at Peleliu.

Colonel Nakagawa realised that almost everything was against him. The Americans would have an enormous naval advantage and total control of the air; their invasion fleet could not be intercepted and destroyed. The intelligence staff were uncertain of where the enemy would strike – the northern island of Babelthuap, the capital Koror, or Peleliu. General Inoue had to keep large reserves on Babelthuap and Koror in case the Americans were planning to invade the whole archipelago, but once the enemy arrived their overwhelming naval and air superiority meant that the chances of shifting Japanese units to reinforce threatened sectors were slim. Nakagawa was aware that his regimental artillery and firepower in general would be inferior to that of the enemy; and the M4 Shermans of the Marines' divisional tank battalion easily outclassed the much lighter Japanese *Ha-Go* tanks, of which the garrison had only about a dozen anyway.

Nevertheless, the Japanese commander did enjoy some significant advantages. The geography of the island virtually dictated where the Americans would land – the stretch of coastline on the south-west of Peleliu, close to the airfield. The colonel accepted that the airfield could not be held for long; but just north and north-west of it was an area known as the Umurbrogol Mountains. 'Mountains' is a grandiose title for a feature whose maximum height was only some 550 feet above sea level; in reality the Umurbrogol was a heavily-wooded, coral-based outcrop of valleys, limestone cliffs, crags, ravines and ridges. Centuries of howling typhoons and torrential rains had turned it into a labyrinth of stone; and then there were the caves – hundreds of natural hiding places, to which the Japanese were to add hundreds more.

Earlier in the year the Americans had taken many aerial photographs of the whole island, and in June US Navy submarines had stood offshore and photographed the planned landing beaches. From this information detailed maps and contoured models were produced to familiarise the Marines with the island prior to the attack. The Umurbrogol was shown as an area of tree-covered uplands, with no indication of the rocky chaos that lay hidden under cover of this foliage. In US planning reports of the time the whole of Peleliu was classified as 'low and flat' – a tragic error that was to have serious repercussions as the battle progressed.

In the short time available to him, Col. Nakagawa made full use of the wild and rocky terrain of the Umurbrogol. Caves were dug and blasted out of the hills to extend and supplement those already provided by nature. It was here, amongst the ridges and gullies which occupied an area just over a mile long by half a mile wide along the north-west edge of Peleliu, that he intended to make his last stand. His aim was not victory, nor survival for his men. The battle of attrition which Nakagawa was planning was to usher in Japan's utterly negative new theory of defence: simply, that if they killed sufficiently huge numbers of the enemy before they themselves were killed, the Americans would eventually sicken of the slaughter and sue for peace. Once the Marines – and later the Army – reached the Umurbrogol, the fighting on Peleliu would take on a dimension of savagery which had seldom been seen before, but which was to be the curtain-raiser for Iwo Jima and Okinawa.

CHAPTER 2

Desecrate – Task Force 58 in March 1944

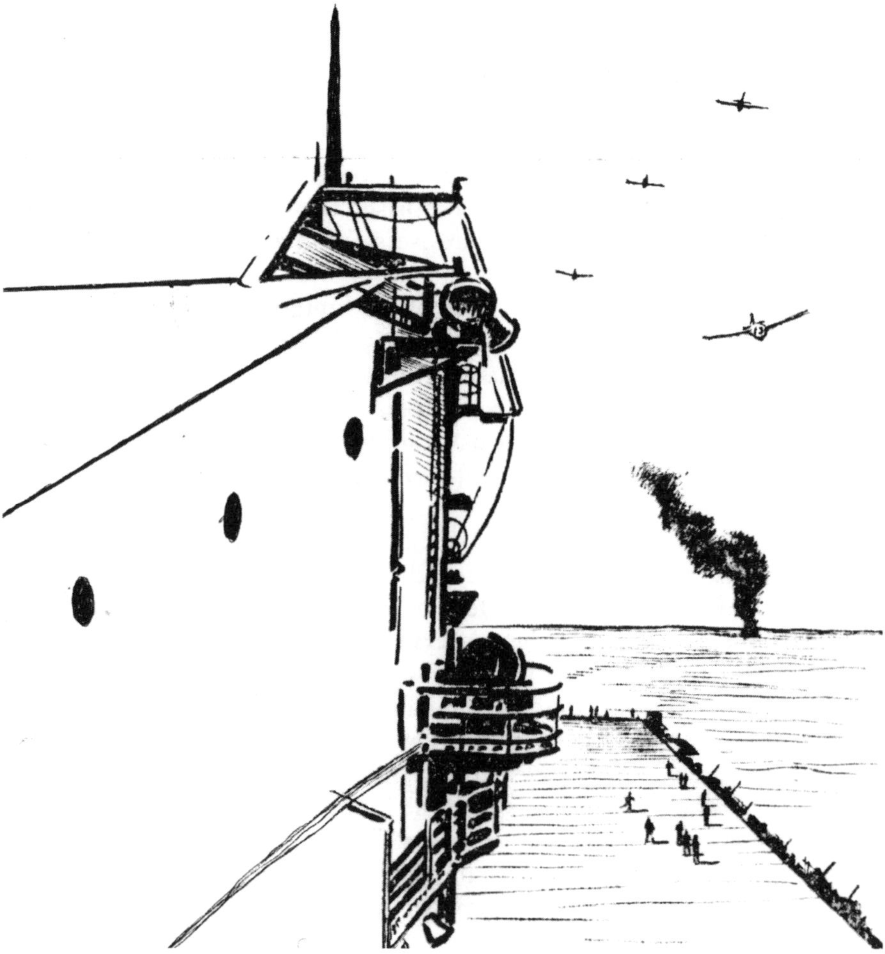

Although separated from the eventual landings on Peleliu by some five months, Task Force 58's preliminary air assault on the Palaus in late March 1944 – code-named Desecrate 1 – was an integral part of the overall US operational plan. For this reason alone it seems fitting to describe it here. Moreover, even a brief summary valuably conveys the flavour of missions which were remote but inseparable from the US Marines' part in the orchestration of amphibious operations.

The Task Force was under the overall command of Adm. Raymond Spruance, Commander 5th Fleet, who flew his flag in the battleship USS *New Jersey*. Spruance could dictate changes in targets as the situation developed; but the Commander Carrier Force, Vice Adm. Mitscher, aboard the USS *Lexington*, controlled the direct tactical deployment of TF58's three component Task Groups, designated 58-1, 58-2 and 58-3. The Task Force had a total strength of no less than 11 aircraft carriers, six battleships, 15 cruisers and 41 destroyers.

The operational plan called for Task Group 58-1, under Rear Adm. J.W.Reeves Jr, to conduct airstrikes on the first day, and then to proceed to Yap the following day. This group was also to maintain protection against possible attacks by Japanese aircraft, and to conduct photographic reconnaissance. Task Group 58-1 comprised the carriers USS *Enterprise, Belleau Wood* and *Cowpens*; the cruisers *Santa Fe, Mobile, Biloxi* and *Oakland*; and 25 destroyers.

Task Group 58-2, under Rear Adm. A.E.Montgomery, was to carry out airstrikes on both days; additionally it was to intercept any surface craft that attempted to leave the Palau lagoons, and to conduct widespread mining operations. The group comprised the carriers *Bunker Hill, Monterey, Hornet* and *Cabot*; the battleships *Iowa* and *New Jersey*; and the cruisers *Wichita, San Francisco, Minneapolis, New Orleans, Boston* and *Baltimore*.

Task Group 58-3, under Rear Adm. S.P.Ginder, was given exactly the same missions as 58-2. It comprised the carriers *Yorktown, Lexington, Princeton* and *Langley*; the battleships *Massachusetts, North Carolina, South Dakota* and *Alabama*; the cruisers *Louisville, Portland, Indianapolis, San Juan,* and the Australian HMAS *Canberra*; and 16 destroyers.

Submarines and destroyers were detailed for 'lifeguard' duties. By this stage of the war the US Navy was devoting considerable resources to recovering aircrew who survived crash-landings or parachute escapes, with submarines and surface vessels stationed along the outward and return routes of airstrikes; the floatplanes catapulted from battleships and cruisers also played a significant part in such rescues. These precautions were valuable in boosting the morale of the carrier aircrews; more coldly, they were worthwhile in safeguarding the Navy's investment in highly trained and skilled specialists who could not easily be replaced. (Total recovery of aircrew during Desecrate 1 was listed as 26 men out of a total of 44 missing – a high rate of rescue, considering that a number of aircraft crashed with the loss of all the crew.)

The attacks on Truk in February had highlighted the advantage of widespread fighter sweeps in advance of the dive-bombers and torpedo-bombers, to suppress enemy opposition over the target area. This was adopted with great success during Desecrate 1, with F6F Hellcat fighters engaging Japanese aircraft in the air before going on to strafe those dispersed around the airfields. The SB2C Helldiver and SBD Dauntless dive-bombers and TBF Avenger torpedo-bombers had the task of attacking the shipping in the Palau harbours and lagoons as their primary targets, with airfields and other ground installations as secondary targets. The principal anchorages were at Urukthapel and Komebail, with smaller sites at Malakal, Iwayami Bay and Rock Islands.

Mine-laying operations had a high priority during the operation, to prevent shipping from escaping and to inhibit the future use of the harbours. In preparation for the forthcoming Stalemate operation, extensive photo reconnaissance – particularly of beaches and reefs around the islands – was also a priority.

Task Group 58-1

As the Task Group headed towards the Palau Islands on 29 March after conducting strikes against Ulithi, Ngulu and Woleai, a patrol of eight Hellcat fighters lifted off the deck of the fleet carrier USS *Enterprise* into a perfect tropical sky. Some 20 miles ahead of the mass of carriers, cruisers and destroyers they spotted a single Mitsubishi G4M 'Betty' twin-engined bomber flying at a mere 100 feet above the calm sea; its near-zero altitude had prevented its being picked up by the *Enterprise*'s radar. Four of the stubby radial-engined fighters, led by Lt. Marks, piled on the power and dived from 6,000 feet into the attack. The first pass seemed inconclusive, but as they started their second run flames poured out of the starboard wing and the bomber plunged into the sea. Amazingly, one of the crew survived the terrific impact and clung to the wreckage, waving at the American pilots who were circling above. It was obvious that the arrival of the various elements of Task Force 58 in the western Carolines must now be assumed to be known to the Japanese.

Group 58-1 rendezvoused with the two other units of the Task Force on 30 March, and a pre-dawn launch from the carriers *Enterprise, Belleau Wood* and *Cowpens* headed for the primary target, the airfield on Peleliu.

Diving in low through a weak barrage of anti-aircraft gunfire, they strafed the airfield hangars and adjacent buildings and destroyed five or six 'Betty' bombers which were dispersed around the perimeter. Most Japanese aircraft lacked the self-sealing fuel tanks fitted by the Allies, and were notorious for catching fire: a pilot's report says that these aircraft 'blazed furiously' as the Hellcats wheeled away and headed north.

The group overflew the harbour at Urukthapel and reported many ships at anchor; over Babelthuap they buzzed the unfinished airfield, before turning back to Peleliu. During their first attack they had wondered at the absence of enemy fighters, but on their return a number of Mitsubishi A6M Zeros were in the air and waiting for them. As the formation split up a series of dogfights developed, in which five of the Hellcats sustained minor damage and three Zeros were shot down. On their return to the carriers a number of pilots complained that their machine guns were malfunctioning; an investigation traced a faulty batch of ammunition on one of the carriers, and this was rectified by the ordnance crews.

The second wave of aircraft – Hellcats, Dauntless dive-bombers and Avenger torpedo-bombers – headed for Kossol Passage, where several ships were reported to be attempting to head for the open sea. In perfect visibility, the group leader saw the long, chalky wake of a destroyer across the deep blue surface, and ordered the Hellcats down to attack. Screaming in at wave-top height with their six 0.50cal machine guns blazing, the fighters silenced the weak anti-aircraft fire from the destroyer and caused extensive fires on the deck; a combination of Dauntless and Avenger attacks rapidly dispatched the blazing warship. Two much smaller ships were seen a little to the west and they too were strafed; one, evidently an ammunition ship, vanished in a huge explosion and the other was left blazing.

Another ship, reported as a destroyer, was intercepted south-west of the Toagel Mlungui Passage by Dauntless dive-bombers, which split into two groups and attacked out of the sun. One bomb is reported to have fallen just short of the bow but the others were misses. One Dauntless made its dive but never pulled out; the pilot must have fallen victim to the destroyer's AA fire, as it plunged into the sea in a great fireball. The destroyer, later identified as the *Wakatake*, was later sunk by aircraft from the carrier *Yorktown* of Task Group 58-3.

Twelve Avengers from the *Enterprise* were launched within seven minutes – remarkable teamwork from the carrier's deck crew. Some of the planes carried torpedoes and others fragmentation bombs; over Babelthuap they split into separate groups, the bombers attacking warehouses and military installations at Koror while the torpedo planes went for the shipping. In this sweep Avengers also dropped bombs with delayed fuzes on and around Peleliu airfield. For the Japanese engineers, trying to keep the runway in service became a game of Russian roulette as violent explosions shook the airfield throughout the night.

In strikes from the carriers *Belleau Wood* and *Cowpens* the seaplane base at Arakabesan was shot up, and two minelayers docked nearby were seen to erupt in brown smoke as mines or depth charges went up. In the Western Lagoon four Hellcats started a strafing attack on a large ship, but just in time the pilots saw red crosses painted on the side and veered away. Two hospital ships were on station in the Palaus, the *Muro Maru* and the *Takasago Maru*, and this was obviously one of them. (It should perhaps be pointed out that as a fixed policy the Japanese did not recognise the protection of the Geneva cross when attacking Allied forces.)

These were the last strikes by Task Group 58-1, which now headed north-west and prepared for operations against Ulithi and Yap.

Task Group 58-2

Sailing with this group were the US Navy's two newest, fastest and most powerful battleships, the 48,000-ton USS *Iowa* and *New Jersey.* It was from the latter that Adm. Spruance was keeping a keen eye on the progress of Desecrate 1. As with Task Group 58-1, the Japanese were aware of the movements of the group; as evening approached on 29 March a radar contact was made, and Hellcats were launched to investigate. An unconfirmed number of G4M 'Betty' bombers were intercepted and one was shot down, the crew being picked up by the destroyer screen the following day.

It emerged that the intruders were based on Truk; and as dawn broke on the 30th, a larger formation of G4Ms appeared from the east and soon registered on radar. Relatively slow, weakly armed, and with their vulnerable unprotected fuel tanks, the bombers presented easy targets; Hellcats from the four carriers in the group had few problems downing ten of the intruders, while the remainder departed hastily for Truk.

Avengers from the torpedo squadrons aboard *Bunker Hill* and *Hornet* carried out mining operations on the 30th. The main concentrations of mines were laid around Arakabesan Island, Ngargol Island, Malakal Passage and Ngell Channel, the most frequently used waterways.

In the afternoon a major dogfight erupted over Peleliu airfield as Hellcats from *Bunker Hill* mixed with 12 Zeros at 3,000 feet; one US fighter pilot crash-landed in the sea close to the shores of Angaur. He was seen to climb out onto the plane's wing and a rescue vessel was alerted to the scene, but he was never found. Another Hellcat, while strafing the airfield, was jumped by a Zero who set his external 'belly tank' on fire. With flames belching from the ruptured tank, the pilot calmly banked his fighter and dumped the blazing container on to the airfield outbuildings.

On the last sortie of the day the Hellcat pilots reported a shortage of targets: all the ships that they could see in the anchorage were either sunk, heavily damaged or beached.

During pre-dawn launches from the *Hornet*, pilots had complained about the close proximity of other carriers – aircraft from other units were appearing as if from nowhere and forcing them off course. Carriers were obliged to allow 10 square kilometres ahead to facilitate circling and formating of departing aircraft; this clearly was not happening, and as a result there were a number of cases of aircraft mistakenly joining up with formations from other carriers.

Accidents during take-off and landing were frequent during carrier operations. One Avenger roared off the end of the flight deck of the *Hornet*, dipped, failed to recover, plunged into the sea, and was torn in two by the bows of the huge ship. By some miracle the pilot was unharmed and was picked up by an escorting destroyer. Another Avenger clipped the 'island' – the towering superstructure on the port side of the carrier's flight deck – pivoted over the No.2 5in anti-aircraft gun, and cartwheeled into the sea; the plane sank rapidly, but all three crew were rescued.

A major flying exploit was achieved by the pilot of another *Hornet*-based Avenger. While carrying out a torpedo attack on a Japanese ship (later identified as the *Iro*) the TBF was hit by accurate anti-aircraft gun fire which damaged the right aileron.

The Avenger barely cleared the ridge at Uruktapel; then the left fuel tank burst into flames, and black smoke began to billow from the engine, which had also been damaged. Luckily the fuel tank self-sealed and the fire died out, and by skilful manipulation of his badly damaged controls and spluttering engine the pilot not only returned to the *Hornet* but made a perfect landing.

There was still plenty of fight left in the Japanese defenders despite the battering that Task Force 58 was giving to all areas of the Palaus. Over Peleliu airfield Lt. Houston, piloting a lumbering Helldiver bomber, was hit by gunfire, and other pilots saw sheets of flame coming from his open bomb bay as the SB2C rapidly lost altitude. As the flames spread the pilot and his gunner bailed out while their plane headed out to sea and crashed in flames. Both crewmen landed in the sea about 100 yards off the south-east coast of Peleliu, but they were never recovered – two more young men listed as missing in action.

A bizarre incident occurred on the same day when four Hellcats, flying as escort to a Kingfisher floatplane engaged on rescue duties, were forced to drive off other 'friendly' US Navy fighters which failed to recognise the flimsy Kingfisher and came in to attack it. (To be fair, Japanese floatplanes were far more common in the Pacific than their American equivalents; there was even a floatplane conversion of the Zero fighter.)

The light carrier *Cabot* was principally engaged in anti-submarine patrols and combat air patrols; and just before sunset on 30 March a flight of her fighters were vectored to investigate a radar contact. They came across nine enemy aircraft, a mixture of Aichi D4Y 'Judy' dive-bombers and Nakajima B6N 'Jill' attack bombers. All were shot down. A reminder that the Pacific war was pitiless on both sides occurred when Hellcats from the carrier *Monterey*, patrolling off the west coast of Angaur, saw a Japanese freighter sinking by the stern; they strafed and sank a fully-laden lifeboat from the ship.

Task Group 58-3

The usual pre-dawn Japanese intruders were in evidence on 29 March, and four of them were shot down by US night-fighters.

Early on the 30th, the USS *Lexington*, Adm. Mitscher's flagship, launched 16 Avengers on a major mine-laying mission. These mines were 'self-arming' and would be expected to remain active for at least four months; but in fact the harbours and anchorages of the Palaus would be sealed for a much longer period. A wide variety of mines were sewn, and the Japanese were at a loss as to how to tackle them; their knowledge of sophisticated mines was non-existent and there were no minesweepers anywhere in the islands.

One of the Dauntless dive-bomber pilots had a remarkable experience. While he was making a diving attack the bomb prematurely detached itself from the SBD's belly shackle and, accelerating faster than the plane, passed through the propeller disc and sheared off 8 inches from all three blades. It did not explode, however, and the pilot successfully returned to his carrier for a new propeller.

Less fortunate was a Hellcat pilot who overshot the arrester wires and barrier, shunting into a parked F6F; both fell down the forward elevator shaft onto a third Hellcat below. The pilot of the third plane was killed instantly and the other two were seriously injured.

Japanese anti-aircraft fire was still posing a serious threat. One Dauntless was hit by a shell that exploded in the cockpit, badly wounding the pilot, William Bailey, in the leg. Bailey was losing a great deal of blood when his gunner/radioman, Harry Kelly, pulled him out of the way and took over the controls, at the same time bandaging the pilot's leg and stopping the bleeding. Given the 'tandem' positions of the pilot's and gunner's stations in the SBD Dauntless, this was a remarkable feat by itself. Over Angaur Island, Bailey recovered sufficiently to regain the controls, and landed the aircraft on the nearest carrier – the *Enterprise* from 58-1. He collapsed immediately upon coming to a halt, being rushed to the sick bay for a blood transfusion and attention to his mangled leg. Both men were later to receive commendations.

On 30 March, 11 Avengers from the *Yorktown* made a 200-mile sweep to the west of the Palaus looking for enemy shipping. Some time into the sortie a ship was spotted from an altitude of 10,000 feet, making tight circles. The bombers circled twice and decided to attack, dropping two 2,000lb bombs, one of which was a near miss while the other fell wide. This turned out to be an unfortunate case of mistaken identity: the ship was the US submarine *Tunny*, on patrol to rescue downed aircrew. The submarine skipper had to make an emergency dive, and his boat sustained sufficient damage to force her to return to Pearl Harbor for repairs. The Commander Submarine Force Pacific Fleet (COMSUBPAC), Vice Adm. 'Uncle Charlie' Lockwood, was furious over this incident, and ordered an investigation which resulted in the flight leader being reprimanded.

The light carrier USS *Princeton* contributed 12 aircraft for initial fighter sweeps and launched anti-submarine and combat air patrols during Desecrate 1. On this occasion she suffered no losses; but the inherent danger of carrier operations would be tragically underlined seven months later, when the *Princeton* was attacked by a Japanese aircraft off the coast of Luzon. A single bomb penetrated to the hangar deck, crammed with aircraft, fuel and munitions, and started uncontrollable fires. The cruiser *Birmingham* came alongside to add her water hoses to the firefighting effort, but a tremendous explosion ripped off the *Princeton's* stern and moved the *Birmingham* 15 feet sideways in the water. The cruiser was peppered with hundreds of steel shards; most of her crew were topside, and no less than 227 were killed or died of their wounds, in addition to 108 members of the crew of the *Princeton*; more than 600 men from the combined crews were injured. This single incident caused more American casualties than in the whole of the battle of Midway.

* * *

Task Force 58's two-day foray into the Palaus had been an overwhelming success and virtually eliminated the Japanese naval and air force presence forever. Over 110 Japanese aircraft were claimed destroyed in the air and a further 214 on the ground – these figures were later disputed as being excessive, but when the Marines invaded in September the only evidence of Japan's Air Flotilla 26 which they saw were dozens of wrecked and burned-out aircraft littering the airfield on Peleliu. If the claims for aircraft destroyed were overestimated, the claims for shipping were if anything too low. Apart from the two hospital ships, every single Japanese vessel in the Palaus was either sunk, severely damaged or beached. The Imperial Navy was forced to abandon all hope of establishing the Palaus as their next line of defence after the loss of Truk, and moved their headquarters to Tawitawi, from where they were to make their final rendezvous with the US Navy at the battle of Leyte Gulf.

The US Navy had proved that in a mere two-day operation they could neutralise the Japanese naval and air force presence in an entire island group. More importantly, the enemy knew that any attempt to replenish these forces would result in another, and possibly more devastating, retaliation. It is true that there was still a powerful Imperial Army presence in the Palaus, but the US Navy had ensured that they were going nowhere. The major objective of Stalemate 2 was to neutralise any threat to Gen. MacArthur's eastern flank during his proposed invasion of the Philippines; but this had already been accomplished by Desecrate 1.

* * *

On the evening of 31 March, Adm. Koga, C-in-C Japanese Combined Fleet, left Koror in an 'Emily' flying boat, intent on moving his flag to Davao Island in the southern Philippines; he was of the opinion that the US Navy attacks were intended to soften up the Palaus' defences prior to an imminent amphibious landing. At some time during the four-hour flight, Koga's flying boat ran into a tropical storm and vanished; no sign of the aircraft or the admiral was ever found.

CHAPTER 3

The Old Breed

In the British Army the oldest regiment of the Line, tracing their unbroken lineage back to 1633, are the Royal Scots – once numbered as the 1st Regiment of Foot; and their proud nickname is 'Pontius Pilate's Bodyguard'. A similar pride inspires the 1st Division of the United States Marine Corps – 'The Old Breed' – heirs to a proud tradition dating back to the War of Independence in the 1770s.

When Japan launched its attack on Pearl Harbor in December 1941 the 1st Division numbered a mere 7,389 officers and enlisted men – roughly a third of its establishment; but patriotic fervour and a vigorous recruiting campaign soon swelled the numbers, and by May 1942 the division was up to its full complement of around 19,000 all ranks. As already mentioned, the core of the division was its three infantry regiments – the 1st, 5th and 7th Marines – each with three battalions (identified in this text as e.g. 1/5th for 1st Battalion, 5th Marine Regiment).

The internal organisation of the division's riflemen and their heavy support weapons evolved steadily during the war, and by September 1944 the USMC had adopted a flexible system which allowed for maximum initiative by small units in combat, and which made the crew-served support weapons available as far down the chain of command as possible. The basic 'building blocks' were the levels between the rifle squads and the infantry battalion to which they belonged. The equipment and task of each sub-unit – indeed, each man – was laid down in neat tables. In battle, of course, the inevitable casualties, loss or destruction of kit, and confusion soon meant that small groups of men found themselves using whatever means were to hand to do the jobs that immediately confronted them, under the leadership of whoever had the skill and courage to seize the initiative.

Each Marine and his buddies belonged to a rifle squad. At full strength the squad consisted of a sergeant and a dozen men, divided into three 'fire teams'; in each team one man carried a fully automatic Browning Automatic Rifle (BAR) and the others semi-automatic rifles, carbines and grenades. Three squads plus a small HQ element made up a rifle platoon of 45-plus men, led by a second lieutenant. Three rifle platoons, plus a machine gun platoon with 12 0.30cal guns, made up a company of just over 230 men, led by a captain; the company headquarters element included a 60mm mortar platoon.

Three rifle companies and a headquarters made up a battalion, just over 1,000 strong and commanded by a lieutenant-colonel backed by two majors. At battalion HQ level were grouped further heavy weapons, which could be divided up and attached to companies and platoons as the situation demanded – 81mm mortars, 2.36in rocket launchers ('bazookas'), flamethrowers and demolition charges. The battalion was usually the highest level in the hierarchy with which an individual Marine felt identified: he belonged to, for instance, the '1st of the 5th', and was convinced that while all Marine units were superior to any Army battalion, the 1/5th Marines were the best unit in the Corps.

Three battalions made up a regiment of more than 3,000 men, led by a full colonel; further heavy assets and specialised equipment were held under the regimental commander's control, including anti-tank guns. The organising principle was that at each level from company HQ upwards to division and beyond, the commanding officer of that level controlled not only his subordinate rifle units, but also a central 'pool' of specialist men and equipment, which he could divide up and attach to the smaller units and sub-units further down the chain according to battlefield need.

Supporting the three infantry regiments were all the other components of the 1st Marine Division which enabled it to fight more or less self-sufficiently. The integral Marine Artillery Regiment, the 11th, had four battalions, two each of 75mm 'pack' howitzers and 105mm howitzers; each battalion had three six-gun batteries. The 1st Marine Tank Battalion had four companies each of 15 M4 Sherman tanks. Supplementing the fighting units were other specialists whose tasks were not primarily to use weapons, but who were often as exposed to danger as the riflemen: battalions of engineers, medical personnel (provided by US Navy Hospital Corpsmen), and transport drivers with jeeps, trucks and amphibious tractors ('Amtracs'). Other unglamorous but essential services were grouped under divisional headquarters – communications, ordnance, supply, clerks, cooks, military police, 'war dogs' – even musicians. The division was a complex, carefully balanced miniature army almost 20,000 strong.

* * *

The commander of the 1st Marine Division in 1942 was Maj.Gen. Alexander Archer Vandegrift, a First World War veteran who was highly regarded in Washington. 'Archie' Vandegrift would lead the division through the gruelling battles of Guadalcanal and Cape Gloucester before being promoted to Commandant of the Marine Corps.

By the end of May 1942, Vandegrift and his Marines were on their way to Wellington in New Zealand. Upon arrival he was summoned to the headquarters of Vice Adm. Robert Ghormley, Commander South Pacific Area, where he learned that the Joint Chiefs of Staff had ordered the 1st Division to occupy the island of Guadalcanal in the British Solomon Islands, where the Japanese had landed and were constructing an airfield (later named Henderson Field, after a pilot killed in the battle of Midway).

Initially, this Operation Watchtower looked like a walk-over; by nightfall on D-Day, 7 August 1942, over 10,000 men were ashore, complete with their M3 Stuart light tanks and artillery, on a 4-mile-long beachhead, without opposition apart from a few bursts of small arms fire.

Much of the credit for the Marines' successful landing must go to a group of 'coast watchers' – British, Australian and New Zealand volunteers, mostly civilians, who had remained on dozens of Pacific islands after the Japanese occupation to provide intelligence of the enemy's location, troop strength and movements. On Guadalcanal a three-man group led by British Cambridge graduate Martin Clemens had provided Vandegrift with vital information about the best location for the landings, the whereabouts of the main Japanese garrison, and the progress of the airfield construction.

Vandegrift overran the airfield on the second day; simultaneously the nearby islands of Florida, Tulagi, Gavutu and Tanambogo were assaulted by four Marine battalions under his second-in-command, Brig.Gen. Rupertus. It was during the occupation of these adjacent islands that some officers of the 1st Division became concerned about the quality of Rupertus' leadership. Florida was taken easily, but on Tulagi, Gavutu and Tanambogo the Marines encountered much stiffer resistance, in a foretaste of what was to happen on Guadalcanal. At the height of the operation Vandegrift received a message from Rupertus in terms that bordered on panic. He reported 60 per cent casualties in his Parachute Battalion (at that time an integral part of the division), and demanded immediate reinforcements. In reality the battalion had taken about 10 per cent casualties, and the whole force had lost only 141 men in wresting the islands from a Japanese garrison estimated at over 1,500. One of Rupertus' battalion commanders contemptuously announced, 'He sat on his ass while the others did the work'.

The Japanese were not slow in reacting to the American landings on Guadalcanal; bombers and fighters were soon on their way to attack the troopships and supply vessels of Adm. Turner's invasion force, and on the night of 8 August a squadron of Imperial Navy cruisers – as skilled in night-fighting as their Army comrades – devastated the American naval forces protecting the beachhead. After a hectic half-hour battle off Savo Island three US Navy cruisers – the *Quincy, Astoria* and *Vincennes* – together with the Australian cruiser HMAS *Canberra*, lay at the bottom of the aptly named Iron Bottom Sound. Admiral Fletcher, commander of the supporting carrier force comprising the *Enterprise, Saratoga* and *Wasp*, on station to provide air cover for the Marines, hastily departed on the pretext that he was 'seriously short of fuel', and the Marines on the islands were left to their own devices. To this day there are many veterans of

Guadalcanal who declare that they were abandoned, and in their eyes Fletcher's reputation never recovered.

In his decisive manner, Adm. Nimitz relieved Ghormley of his South Pacific command and appointed Vice Adm. William 'Bull' Halsey in his place. Halsey flew into Guadalcanal and made a personal assessment of the situation; within weeks supplies of food, fuel, ammunition and aircraft were steadily making their way to the hungry and disease-ridden Marines. Marine airman Brig.Gen. Roy Geiger arrived, and his flyers operating from the perilous airstrip of Henderson Field were soon dubbed the 'Cactus Air Force', after Guadalcanal's codename. Flying a mixture of carrier fighters and P-38 Lightning twin-engine fighters scrounged from the Marines, Army Air Force and Navy, they eventually destroyed more than 420 Japanese aircraft and sank ten transport ships.

From his HQ on Bougainville the commander of the Japanese 17th Army, Lt.Gen. Harukichi Myakutake, ordered Maj.Gen. Kiyotake Kawaguchi to retake Guadalcanal with his 6,000-strong 35th Brigade. The first unit ashore was a battalion of the 28th Infantry Regiment led by Col. Kyono Ichiki. On the night of 21/22 August they hurled themselves against the 2/1st Marines, dug in along the Ilu River, in frenzied but vain charges. This Japanese underestimation of the Marines cost them almost the whole of Ichiki's battalion.

On 12–14 September, in what became known as the battle of 'Bloody Ridge', Kawaguchi's force repeatedly attacked the heights overlooking Henderson Field; but the meagre Marine force, under the command of the Raider Battalion's Lt.Col. 'Red Mike' Edson, repelled constant assaults until Kawaguchi's force, reduced by at least 1,500, fled into the jungle. After this victory the Marines went onto the offensive. In September Rear Adm. Turner guided a seven-ship convoy through Iron Bottom Sound and, under air cover from the Cactus Air Force, disembarked the division's 7th Regiment together with tanks, artillery, ammunition and supplies.

The Japanese were still determined to overrun the Marine beachhead, however, and by 19 October reinforcements had brought their forces on the island up to some 20,000 – mostly from their 2nd Infantry Division, with strong artillery and some tanks. On 22 October they began launching attacks across the Mataniko River; although these were badly co-ordinated, the necessary shifting of units in the perimeter left the 1/7th Marines led by 'Chesty' Puller, and a battalion from the Army's 164th Infantry, alone on Bloody Ridge when a massive night attack hit them. In an intense two-day struggle on 24–25 October more than 3,000 of the estimated 8,500 Japanese attackers were killed; Marine fatalities were 63 men.

Later, elements of the 2nd Marine Division and Army units arrived and the tide turned inexorably against the Japanese.

In early December 1942 the 'Old Breed' began leaving Guadalcanal; casualties had been heavy, but far more Marines had been laid low by sickness – malaria and other fevers, fungal diseases, malnutrition, dysentery and a host of other tropical maladies had accounted for many more Marines than did Japanese bullets. In February 1943 US forces reached Cape Esperance at the western end of Guadalcanal, but the last of the enemy had fled, evacuated during the night.

Acts of heroism were recognised: among a number of men awarded the Medal of Honor were 'Red Mike' Edson of the Raiders, for the first battle of Bloody Ridge; and Gunnery Sgt. John Basilone of the 1/7th, who was credited with over 100 Japanese killed on the night of 24 October. ('Manila John' Basilone was sent back to America to boost the War Bond drive, but soon tired of the rounds of parties and speeches. He would return to the Pacific with the 5th Division, only to die on the beaches of Iwo Jima.)

* * *

What happened next did not please 'Archie' Vandegrift one little bit. From Guadalcanal his exhausted Marines were shipped to Brisbane, Australia, to become part of Gen. MacArthur's command. Subordination to an Army general did not sit well with the 1st Division 'leathernecks'; but MacArthur was desperately short of men, and the 1st Division was available.

What the Army had not anticipated was the appalling state in which the division arrived. Disease-ridden, worn out, and short of equipment and replacements, they were in no condition to fight anybody. A USMC officer who watched some of them disembark recorded: 'The men were ragged, still dirty, thin, anaemic, shallow, listless. Just about one out of every ten of them fell down, tumbling limply down the steep ladder on their backs . . .'.

The stop-over in Brisbane was brief, and the division was dumped in a flat, swampy area 15 miles outside the city. Vandegrift sought a meeting with MacArthur and told him flatly that his men needed a suitable site in which to recover and re-equip before they could be considered battle-ready once more. MacArthur apologised and admitted that he had not anticipated the situation; within days they were heading for Melbourne, where they were treated as heroes by the townsfolk.

The initial period of rest and relaxation gradually gave way to a strict regime of training as replacements poured in from the 'Boot Camps' in America. MacArthur had wanted the 'Old Breed' for Operation Cartwheel, an assault on the Japanese forces massing in New Guinea for an invasion of northern Australia, but rebuilding the division would take too long.

It was at this time that Maj.Gen. Vandegrift was recalled to Washington, where President Roosevelt had two surprises for him: the award of the Medal of Honor for his defence of Guadalcanal, and promotion to the top appointment in the Marine Corps – the Commandant. Vandegrift returned to Melbourne in March 1943, to find his men in much better shape; his only remaining task was to turn over command of the division to Rupertus, now promoted to major-general and awarded the Navy Cross for 'bravery and leadership on Tulagi during the Guadalcanal campaign'.

William H.Rupertus was a dour, moody and uncommunicative man who inspired little confidence in his staff or his men (the Leathernecks had labelled him 'Rupe the Stupe'). Aged 55 at the time of Peleliu, he had served in the 'Banana Wars' and in China in the 1930s. It was in China that he had lost his first wife and two children to a scarlet fever epedemic. To what extent that tragedy coloured his personality is unclear; but it is known that he was subject to profound mood swings, and formed deep-seated likes and dislikes for individual members of his staff.

* * *

In July 1943 the division was earmarked for a future operation against Cape Gloucester on the island of New Britain, where a Japanese airfield threatened the flank of the Allied advance towards the Philippines. Leaving Melbourne in late October for Milne Bay in New Guinea, the division trained for beach landings with the new family of specialist landing craft which were now becoming available. As the folks at home were celebrating Christmas Day 1943, the 1st Marine Division were sweating out the approaching landings off the swampy north-western coast of New Britain. The landing was scheduled for 7.30am on the following day, and again the luck of the 'Old Breed' held. The preliminary naval bombardment and bombing proved a needless exercise, as Japanese opposition was virtually non-existent and within an hour 5,000 Marines were ashore. That afternoon it began raining; and it continued raining for five more days.

James W.Johnston, a machine-gunner with the 5th Regiment, was experiencing his first taste of action. He had sailed to Melbourne in the liberty ship *Mormac Wren* as one of the host of replacements filling the gaps in the ranks after the Guadalcanal campaign. After a short period at Camp Balcolm near Frankston, he was shipped to New Britain as part of the first assault wave:

'First it was over the side of the transports, down cargo nets under a load that made your legs, arms and lungs burn, so close to maximum effort that you feared that you would fall. Then it was onto the beaches, where the really hard work began. There you would strain your ass off all day through the deep, sticky mud and jungle, then stand watch a third or half the night. Most of the days and nights it rained. What rest you got was generally in a hole full of water.

'Mosquitoes swarmed everywhere. If you swung your arm in a half circle, shoulder high, you would hit several of them. You always had prickly heat bumps. Leeches were everywhere, as were the black, scorpion-like bastards whose sting was so potent. It was a muddy slop hole, the most miserable physical conditions I've ever been in. Lots of pretty tough guys completely crapped out.'

The division's after-action report recorded the result of the continual rain: 'Water backed up in the swamps in the rear of the shoreline, making them impassable for wheeled and tracked vehicles. The many streams which emptied into the sea in the beachhead area became raging torrents. Some even changed course. Troops were soaked to the skin and their clothes never dried during the entire operation.'

When the Marines advanced on the island's airfield the enemy showed some reaction, but by noon on 31 December it was in American hands. However, although a large beachhead around the airfield was soon secured, the Marines now faced long months of exhausting 'cat and mouse' fighting as they pursued Gen. Matsuda's 10,000 Japanese troops through the worst kind of tropical jungle. The enemy showed their usual genius for siting and concealing interlocking systems of gunpits and log bunkers; encounters in the dense rainforest would begin without warning as hidden machine guns ripped into the point squads, and could seldom be brought to a conclusion without waiting for tanks to struggle up and blast the enemy positions with their 75mm guns. Snipers tied themselves into treetops, sometimes waiting until the Marines had passed them before firing from behind. By contrast, occasionally the Japanese would emerge from their emplacements and mount wild *banzai* charges, heedless of casualties.

If this kind of fighting wore down the nerves, by far the worst enemies were the weather and the terrain. Torrential tropical downpours drenched the troops as they hacked their way through the dense undergrowth or struggled waist-deep in slimy swampland. The chafing of wet clothing and web equipment caused ulcerous jungle sores which never seemed to heal; skin diseases were endemic; and, operating miles ahead of the supply units, the men were constantly hungry. Richard Bruce Watkins, then a second lieutenant, recalls life in the Cape Gloucester jungle:

'Because the jungle was so dense, our travel was confined to existing trails and the order of march was necessarily single file. Out in front would be two scouts approximately 20 feet apart, 30 feet back would be the platoon leader, and bringing up the rear would be the platoon sergeant. The scouts were to prevent ambush and alert the main body to any enemy troops in time to react. As I became more knowledgeable, I would exchange places with one of the scouts. I felt it was important for the leader to stick his neck out too, and thus I got a valuable indoctrination when enemy activity was slight.'

These patrols often flared up into fierce encounters with the Japanese: 'We proceeded by LCM to a spot about a mile from Kandoka, [and] we had only gone a short way when our scouts opened up on two Japanese soldiers. Rushing up, I saw both on the ground with Jenkins and Cook standing over them. One of them recovered and I raised my carbine to finish him off. I hesitated, and Sgt. Stasiak said, "Do it", whereupon I put a bullet through the man's head. Jenkins said a little scornfully, "He was already done for", but Stasiak said, "It needed doing." I never hesitated again when dealing with an enemy.'

In April 1944, much to the joy of the Leathernecks, the Army's 41st Division were landed to relieve the Marines and complete the mopping-up of the remaining enemy troops, who had dispersed into the jungle or headed eastward in a desperate attempt to reach Rabaul. Casualties from enemy action during the Cape Gloucester campaign were 311 killed and 1,036 wounded; but casualties from sickness, principally malaria and dysentery, were in the thousands. Many Marines were to suffer for the rest of their lives from tropical diseases contracted in the Cape Gloucester jungles. James W.Johnston again: 'Though I didn't know it then, I was one of New Britain's non-battle casualties. I had begun to have chronic heartburn and indigestion. I didn't know what to do about it, so I just went on with my duties. It was at home, after the war, that I found out what was wrong. I was using the bathroom one morning in Nebraska when it felt like one of my intestines was coming out of my rectum. Our old country doctor came to my house to check it out and found about five feet of worm hanging out of my asshole. Lord only knows how much more there was or had been of that one, or how many different kinds of worms I had to go with him – I had big ones and little ones. From the flies, or mosquitoes, or ticks, or leeches, or the local water, or something, I had one hell of a dose of intestinal parasites.'

* * *

As the Marines dreamed of a much-needed period of rest, recuperation and regrouping, another battle was being fought out far above their weary heads. Delighted with their performance at Guadalcanal and Cape Gloucester, Gen. MacArthur was determined to keep 'his' Marines as part of the 6th Army to spearhead his march through the islands to the Philippines. Admiral Nimitz and Gen. Vandegrift were equally determined to bring them back into the fold of the Marine Corps. The fracas involved the Chiefs of Staff in Washington and aides to the President, and was only resolved by a direct order from Adm. King, Chief of Naval Operations and the Joint Chiefs, to 'release the 1st Marine Division to Naval Command as soon as practicable'. On 4 May 1944 the last of the 'Old Breed' embarked for a destination that even the most knowledgeable among them had never heard of: Pavuvu.

CHAPTER 4

'Here's Pavuvu'

The 1st Marine Division had originally been allocated space on Guadalcanal to prepare for the Peleliu invasion; but now the 3rd Marine Division were there, training for the assault on Guam in the Marianas. Somewhere else had to be found – in a hurry – for the 'Old Breed' to prepare for their next campaign.

The story has it that Pavuvu was chosen by Gen. Roy Geiger when he overflew the island in a PBY Catalina flying boat; if this is true, there are many Marines who would have preferred that he had flown a little lower. Pavuvu, one of the then-British administered Russell Islands, lies some 60 miles west of Guadalcanal; it was previously used by the Unilever Company for the production of copra, but the conglomerate had hastily abandoned the island shortly after the outbreak of the Pacific War. Roughly 10 miles long by 6 miles across, the island had an appealing appearance when viewed from the troopships as they approached Macquitti Bay on the northern shore; the white sandy beaches and coconut palms were reminiscent of the Dorothy Lamour 'South Sea island' films that were so popular at that time. In this case first impressions proved deceptive.

Once the Marines moved a few hundred yards inland they were met by what could only be described as a thinly crusted swamp. There were no lights, and no roads, merely mud-covered tracks; and the promised battalion of 'Seabees' (Navy Construction Battalions) who were expected to build accommodation for the division turned out to be a mere 50 in number – not that numbers were relevant, since there were no materials for them to build anything with.

Many Peleliu veterans remember Pavuvu, even without the Imperial Japanese Army, as being worse than Cape Gloucester. The temperature and humidity were constantly high; tropical downpours were a regular feature, as were mosquitoes and other insect life. And then there were the rats – thousands of them, running through the camps and into the tents. Lieutenant R. Bruce Watkins recalls: 'When the rains let up, the rats came by the thousand [. . . at night they] ran over tents, gear, and us. We sank five-gallon cans in the earth and baited gangplanks over them. The rats would run out on the planks for the bait, drop into three inches of water, and be disposed of later. Many were hit by throwing knives or decapitated with machetes.

'As soon as the rats left, the crabs came, [also] nocturnal; millions of them could be heard rustling over the ground at night. In the morning, boots and blankets had to be emptied of them. Efforts to kill them only resulted in piles of dead ones emitting a fearful stench. Eventually we just let them crawl and have their fun, until they too disappeared as quickly as they came.'

Everywhere, rotting coconuts – the detritus of the copra trade – added to the stink; at one time the Marines formed lines and passed hundreds along to the water's edge where they were dumped into the sea, but the futility of the exercise finally made them give up.

For a long time food consisted of C-rations – dehydrated potatoes, powdered egg and Spam being the mainstay. Bathing facilities were virtually non-existent. The trick was to wait for one of the frequent tropical downpours to start, then dash out into the open and try to soap up, wash, and rinse before the rain stopped – and since the rain stopped as suddenly as it started, there was always an unfortunate group who were left covered in lather, trying to clean up as best they could.

More serious was the lack of space for training. Tons of coral were dug and blasted to pave the mud tracks and make them usable for tanks and other vehicles, and to try to provide parking areas for the 'Amtracs' and DUKWs, artillery and jeeps. However, the whole centre of the island, lined with rows of coconut groves, was merely a thinly covered swamp which could not support any type of vehicle's weight. The Marines were confined to a single peninsula of land in the north of Pavuvu, and it was in this crowded area that manoeuvres, rifle practice, flame-throwing and all other exercises had to be carried out. It was a common sight to see Marines becoming mixed up with other groups as they vied for space on the crowded peninsula.

Morale reached a low point some weeks after the Marines arrived on Pavuvu. Feeling themselves forgotten and maltreated, some went 'Asiatic' – a Marine term for extreme depression, loneliness and boredom, comparable to the Foreign Legion's legendary *'cafard'*. Bizarre behaviour became more noticeable, and there was a disproportionate number of suicides.

'Remember that we didn't have zip for equipment and supplies', writes Oliver Sweetland of the 3rd Armored Amphibian Tractor Battalion. 'The tentage that we received from another part of the Russell Islands was in very poor condition and rotting, the ground was covered in rotting coconuts and palms, and it seemed that a zillion rats lived in the trees – at night they would scamper from tent to tent and back into the trees.

'One of the most humorous things that we had to put up with was the cattle and horses that had been left behind by the Unilever Company. They would wander throughout the tent rows from company to company. These moo-cows were not just your normal farm critters by any means; they had huge sweeping sets of horns, similar to the famed Texas longhorns, and were of a good size and mean temperament to match. [You've] got to remember that they had been wild for at least two years, and some of these bulls would not back down, even for a tank – just try doing tank or infantry manoeuvres with wild critters screwing up the works.'

About 10 miles to the east of the 1st Division base, on the island of Banika, was the Navy's 4th Base Depot. The contrast between this facility and the mudhole that had been scraped out of the coconut groves by the 'Old Breed' was startling. Here were paved roads, permanent buildings, hospitals, cinemas, PXs and even women – Navy nurses and Red Cross workers, all safely quartered in huge barbed wire compounds patrolled by MPs.

It was to Banika that Bob Hope and his group of entertainers came on one of their Pacific tours. When he heard that the 1st Division were on nearby Pavuvu, he insisted that he and a few of his troupe be allowed to give a show for the Marines. Arriving in a few single-engine Stinson Sentinel aircraft which landed on the coral-covered roads, Bob and his companions – singer Frances Langford, comedian Jerry Colonna and dancer Patti Thomas – gave an impromptu show which was the talking-point among the Leathernecks for weeks afterwards.

The front row was of course taken up by the 'brass', including Gen. Rupertus, with the ranks getting progressively lower the further back from the stage. Langford responded to shouts of 'Paper Doll' and sang that popular song of the time; the bug-eyed Colonna rattled out non-stop jokes, and Patti Thomas gave a few delighted Marines dancing lessons before going into a dance routine that raised the already sizzling temperature. At last Hope sang 'Thanks for the Memory', his long-time signature tune, bringing to an end a show that still remains in the memory of many veterans.

'When it was time to leave, they went back to the road that was used for a landing strip and got into their little aircraft', recalls machine-gunner Jim Johnston. 'As it happened, the plane carrying Frances Langford taxied down the road, turned into the wind for take-off, and stopped not more than 50 yards from where I stood alone. She looked out of the window and waved at me – not at five thousand bellowing Marines falling over one another, but at one lonely asshole. She may not have realised that she was waving at just me standing there alone, but I did. I'm sure that she didn't remember it the next day; but even if I were to live ten thousand years I'd never forget it.'

One Marine still treasures a trophy of that day: a photograph taken during the show of Bob sitting next to Gen. Rupertus, and signed, 'Here's Pavuvu – Bob Hope'.

* * *

Painfully slowly, the camp began to take shape. Roads were paved, food supplies improved, wooden decking was fitted into tented areas, and even a makeshift movie screen appeared between two coconut trees.

Many of the Marines who had been in the Pacific since shortly after the start of the war were due to be relieved, and the arrival of nearly 5,000 replacements made this possible. While a blessing for the 260 officers and 4,600 men who rotated back to the States, whether this was a wise policy is seriously open to doubt. Most of the Marines who headed home were toughened, experienced and specialist troops; the replacements were green kids straight from Boot Camp – many had only been in the Corps for a few months, and their average age was 18 to 19 years. No matter how enthusiastic or patriotic they were – and there was no doubt of that – it is doubtful if they were fully prepared for one of the war's fiercest battles.

A vital part of the training programme was the rehearsal for amphibious landings. It must be remembered that although they had been in combat for a year and a half, neither on Guadalcanal nor Cape Gloucester had the 1st Division faced an opposed beach landing operation. A number of sites were considered, but had to be rejected for various reasons. Brigadier-General Oliver Smith, the divisional second-in-command, had conducted aerial surveys of a number of islands; one that had all the attributes of Peleliu had to be discounted because the Australian government were unwilling to evacuate the native population. Eventually it was decided that the Tassafaronga area of Guadalcanal would have to suffice; there was no reef – an essential for a realistic rehearsal – but landings were made with accompanying naval gunfire to try to duplicate the conditions of an actual invasion.

(At around the same time the Army's 81st Division, who had moved out of their training area on Tulagi, also made their own practice landings near Cape Esperance in preparation for their invasion of Angaur.)

Before the manoeuvres at Tassafaronga had even been mounted, Gen. Rupertus disappeared to Washington – an absence that amazed his staff, particularly Oliver Smith. Only weeks before a major amphibious landing it was naturally assumed that the commander would be there overseeing the training, planning and organisation of his division, but for six weeks the reins were left in the hands of Gen. Smith. There has never been a satisfactory explanation for Rupertus' absence, which was unprecedented during the whole of the Pacific War. It has been suggested that Vandegrift, his long-time friend, allowed him home to see his infant son – Rupertus had married for the second time shortly before being shipped out to the Pacific, and had never seen his child. If this explanation is correct it says much for the Commandant's humanity, but less for the judgement of both men.

When Gen. Rupertus returned to Pavuvu, detailed plans for the assault on Peleliu had already been formulated by Oliver Smith and the headquarters staff. It was already becoming evident that the very capable second-in-command was going to shoulder a large part of the responsibility, and make many vital decisions about the conduct of the battle.

Oliver Smith and his 1st Division HQ staff laboured under great difficulties during the preparation of the assault plans. Normally the planning for an operation of this magnitude would have been carried out at Adm. Nimitz's headquarters in Hawaii; but with Adm. Spruance, the mastermind behind most of the Pacific amphibious operations, already heavily involved in the Marianas invasion, the 1st Division HQ and the planners in Hawaii were reduced to a long distance radio dialogue that sometimes bordered on the bizarre. 'We were like jungle tribes talking to each other with tom-toms', recalls one of Oliver Smith's aides.

Even when Gen. Rupertus finally returned from Washington, Smith found it nearly impossible to communicate with him. 'He was aloof, sometimes confusing and restrained', said Smith, who stated that he was only invited to the divisional commander's office when some VIP or other was visiting – 'I was never consulted about anything tactical, or anything like that'. Another obstacle to smooth functioning of the divisional staff came when Gen. Rupertus broke his ankle during training exercises. 'He started to climb into an Amtrac and the hand hold gave way, and he fell backwards onto rough coral rock and badly fractured his ankle – he was in bed for quite a while', recalled Oliver Smith. While such an accident would normally have been only an inconvenience, on the very eve of a major amphibious assault it posed a serious problem. Rupertus did not report the injury that would severely restrict his mobility during the coming battle.

There was no doubt that the 1st Division was in less than prime condition for what was destined to be one of the Pacific War's major battles. Guadalcanal had initially taken a heavy toll in casualties, and the prolonged campaign on New Britain, though not particularly bloody, had been physically exhausting. Conditions on Pavuvu had hardly helped improve the men's morale, fitness or efficiency.

A string of unfortunate accidents dogged preparations for the departure for Peleliu. The battleships USS *California* and *Tennessee*, earmarked as part of the attack force, collided off Guadalcanal and the former had to be withdrawn. Two oil tankers also collided and were sent for repair. Only days before embarkation a destroyer and a troopship collided; the troopship sank, luckily without loss of life. The catalogue of mishaps continued unabated. Seven troop transports, capable of holding over 6,000 Marines, failed to arrive after a mistake in their orders directed them elsewhere; and only two tank landing ships (LSTs) turned up at Pavuvu, which meant that only 30 of the available 46 Shermans were loaded. The 1st Division had been promised 50 DUKWs (amphibious trucks), but they only arrived days before departure. The DUKW was an awkward beast which needed a skilled and experienced driver; but none were supplied, and men from the division's 1st Motor Transport Battalion had to be given a hastily improvised crash course. Even the embarkation of the division presented serious problems. The facilities on Pavuvu were totally inadequate, and about half of the Marines and their equipment would have to leave from either nearby Banika, or Guadalcanal and Tulagi over 60 miles away. The Marines could be excused for thinking that the operation was haunted by a jinx from day one.

* * *

The island of Peleliu was of very irregular outline, but might tenuously be compared to a three-pronged fork pointing to the north-east (see Map 2, page 51). The western or left-hand prong was by far the largest; the majority of the important features and enemy works were found on this prong and on the 'handle' below it. The central prong was much shorter; and the eastern or right-hand prong was extremely narrow and featureless.

The invasion plan drawn up largely by Oliver Smith and his HQ staff was sound, but it threatened few surprises for the Japanese. The very nature of Peleliu's terrain and the reefs around the coast ensured that the selected landing sites in the south-west, on the edge of the 'fork handle', were predictable; consequently, the Marines were sure of a rough reception.

The obvious first objective was the airfield. Constructed in the late 1930s, it had a main runway more than 1,000 yards long, and a shorter intersecting strip at 90 degrees, both paved with crushed coral. Full servicing facilities and hangars were sited near the northern taxiways. North of these lay the main Japanese headquarters and barracks complex.

To the north-west of the airfield lay the Umurbrogol 'Mountains', described in Chapter 1. These features were bounded by roads on either side – the West and East Roads – which converged at the northern end of the island's 'left-hand prong', near to the pre-war Phosphate Refinery. A few hundred yards north of the refinery, a causeway led to the smaller island of Ngesebus, where a small fighter airstrip was under construction. The remainder of Peleliu was largely a mass of mangrove swamps, shoal coral and jungle.

Five landing beaches, each approximately 500 yards long, were chosen to the west of the airfield (see Map 3, page 52). Here the reef's outer edge was between 700 and 800 yards from the shoreline, thus guarding it with nearly half a mile of shallow water over sharp, irregular coral. From north to south they were codenamed White 1, White 2, Orange 1, Orange 2 and

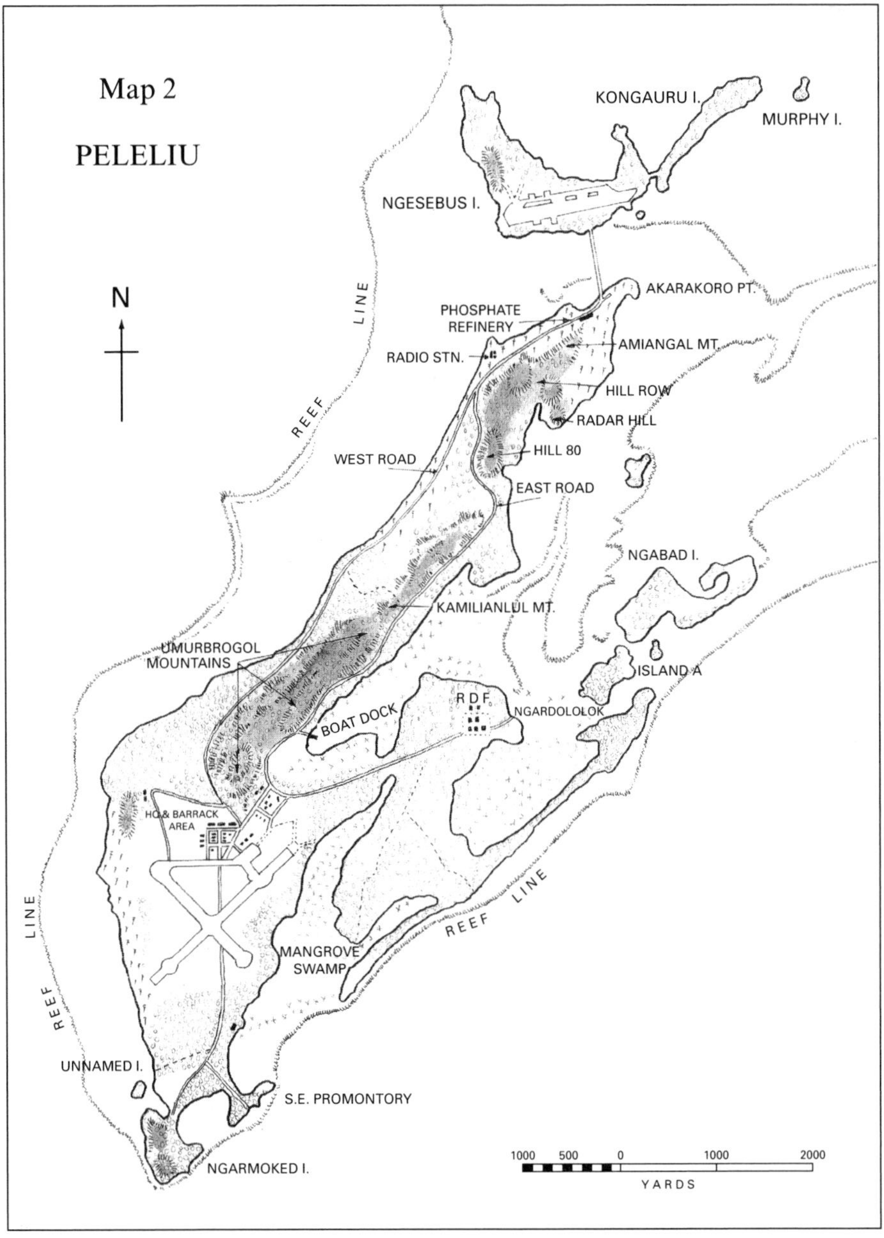
Map 2
PELELIU
N
KONGAURU I.
MURPHY I.
NGESEBUS I.
AKARAKORO PT.
PHOSPHATE REFINERY
AMIANGAL MT.
RADIO STN.
HILL ROW
RADAR HILL
HILL 80
WEST ROAD
EAST ROAD
REEF LINE
NGABAD I.
KAMILIANLUL MT.
UMURBROGOL MOUNTAINS
ISLAND A
R D F
NGARDOLOLOK
BOAT DOCK
HQ & BARRACK AREA
MANGROVE SWAMP
UNNAMED I.
S.E. PROMONTORY
NGARMOKED I.
1000 500 0 1000 2000
YARDS

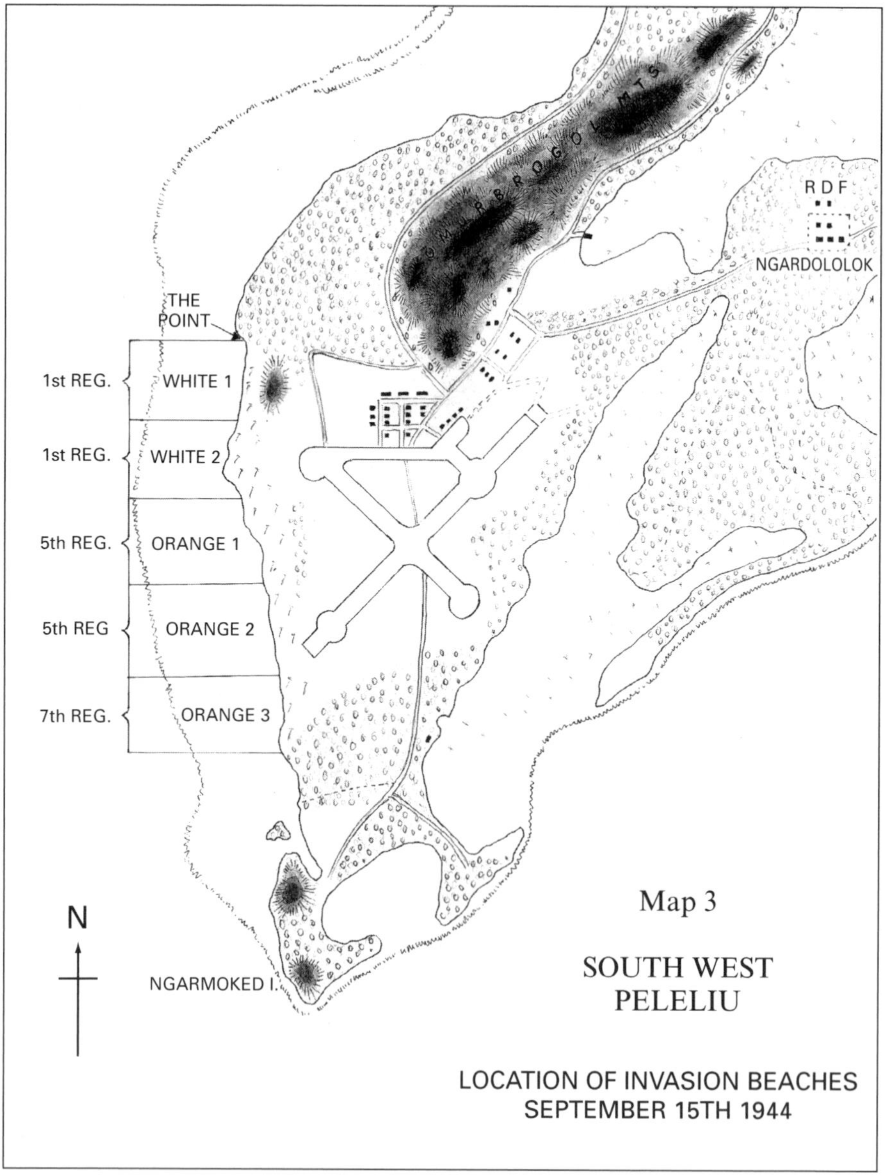

Map 3

SOUTH WEST PELELIU

LOCATION OF INVASION BEACHES SEPTEMBER 15TH 1944

Orange 3. The Marine Corps history of the battle states that: 'A landing on the White and Orange Beaches, followed by a drive straight across the island to seize the airfield and split the defenders, was the scheme of manoeuvre ultimately determined. [Since] none of the remaining beaches which might permit a landing in force would allow the rapid development of an adequate beachhead which is so essential in a landing operation, the correctness of the decision to land on the White and Orange Beaches is hardly open to question'.

Consideration had been given to an area on the south-east of the island which was designated Purple Beach. The reef was no more than 200 yards wide at this point; but the beach gave way immediately to a large, dense area of mangrove swamp, and the only access to the remainder of the island was over a corridor that was barely wide enough for a single road – a bottleneck that the Japanese could be expected to exploit to the full.

The plan called for 'Chesty' Puller's 1st Marine Regiment to land one battalion on each of the White Beaches, with the remaining battalion held in reserve. The 1st Marines would drive inland to the barracks area north of the airfield, and then swing north to the ridges of the Umurbrogol.

Colonel 'Bucky' Harris's 5th Marines, in the centre, would put one battalion on each of Orange Beaches 1 and 2, with the reserve battalion landing one hour later. The troops on Orange 1 would tie in with Puller's men on White 2; the remainder would drive straight ahead to the airfield and then beyond it to the edge of the central mangrove swamp.

The 7th Marines, under Col. 'Hard Head' Hanneken, would leave their 2nd Battalion aboard ship as a floating reserve. The other two battalions would attack Orange Beach 3 'in column' – i.e. one after the other – and press ahead straight to the edge of the mangrove swamp. Once there they would swing south, and mop up the enemy in the south of the island.

The reasons for this scheme were obvious. The division would land on a broad front, onto open ground suitable for tank operations; artillery could easily be landed and deployed in support of the infantry; and the airfield, the principal objective, would be taken early in the battle.

Some of the disadvantages were perhaps not fully appreciated. The Japanese were acutely aware that this was the most desirable landing site, and had made their preparations accordingly. The high ground to the north-west in the foothills of the Umurbrogol – whose tortured terrain was not, as we have seen in Chapter 1, sufficiently detailed on the maps issued to the Marines – provided the Japanese artillery with dominating positions from which the whole of the invasion zone could be swept.

Nor had the thorny questions of reserves and ratios been resolved prior to the attack. Initially the plan had earmarked two-thirds of the Army's 81st Division (less its 323rd Regimental Combat Team) as a floating reserve for the operation, only to be deployed to Angaur when the commanding general decided that they were not required on Peleliu. But these two regiments were later committed to attack Angaur on 17 September, and three days later the 323rd RCT was ordered to Ulithi. Only one battalion of the 7th Marines was to be held in reserve off Peleliu to provide the vital 'second wind' – that counter-punch by fresh troops which gets a stalled attack moving again at the critical place and moment.

During the fighting on Saipan in June/July many documents had been captured by the Americans, including the complete order of battle of the Japanese 31st Army, under whose command the Palau Islands fell. Among these papers was a table of organisation of the Palau garrison. General Rupertus must surely have been aware that his division faced an enemy numbering around 10,000 men, the largest part of them infantry of the 14th Division, war-hardened and brutalised by the long campaigns in China. The two full years of bitter fighting which the US Marine Corps had experienced since they landed on Guadalcanal had taught them, over and again, that well-trained and well-led Japanese infantry were suicidally stubborn in defence and brave in counter-attack; to them, 'death before surrender' was not an empty slogan but an unquestioned tactical principle. At Tarawa, of some 2,600 Imperial Navy infantrymen, just 17 were captured alive, and many were found to have killed themselves in their foxholes and bunkers when all means of resistance was gone.

Although the reinforced 1st Marine Division still had just under 27,000 men to take Peleliu, the vital early stages of the attempt would depend in practice on the front-line infantrymen. The eight rifle battalions in the assault waves totalled only around 9,000 men. Comparing this figure with the known size of the garrison, the ratio of attackers to defenders was reduced, at best, to one-to-one. Accumulated experience from many other island battles showed that successful attackers needed a margin of at least three-to-one. 'Chesty' Puller and Oliver Smith both expressed their concerns; and Smith in particular was alarmed at the prospect of landing with only a solitary battalion in reserve. Yet despite this totally unacceptable ratio, all evidence suggests that Gen. Rupertus was not perturbed.

* * *

And so the eve of the Peleliu operation approached – an undertaking clouded by doubt and indecision from the outset. Admiral Halsey simply did not believe that the landings were necessary. The 'first team' of amphibious experts – Ray Spruance, Kelly Turner and Holland Smith, who together had masterminded the 'island-hopping' campaign across the Pacific – were preoccupied with the invasion of the Marianas, and from there would move directly to the Iwo Jima operation. The assault force was, by all conventional wisdom, insufficiently strong, inadequately rested and rehearsed, and had a large minority of untested boys in its ranks. As worrying were the serious reservations held by many officers about the commanding general of the assault division.

Days before the 1st Division left Pavuvu for Peleliu, Rupertus called a meeting of his officers. 'We're going to have some casualties,' he announced, 'but let me assure you this is going to be a fast one; rough, but fast. We'll be through in three days – it may only take two'. He then continued, 'Someone find and bring me the sword of the Japanese commander on Peleliu.' The assembled officers could only stare at one another in amazement.

David Lloyd George, Britain's Prime Minister during the First World War, had remarked of the Foreign Secretary, Sir Edward Gray: 'The inflexibility of his mind, unqualified by larger knowledge, rendered it easy for him to drift into courses of action which a more imaginative sense and a swifter instinct would question and repudiate.' With the admittedly easy perceptions of hindsight, it is tempting to apply the same judgement to Maj. Gen. William H.Rupertus.

CHAPTER 5

The Tiger's Den

When Col. Kunio Nakagawa and his 2nd Infantry Regiment had moved to Peleliu in April they had thrown themselves into implementing what was called 'The Palau Group Sector Training for Victory Order'. It is worth examining parts of this document in order to appreciate the thinking that lay behind the defence of the island.

The introduction states that on the day of the invasion, the garrison should attempt to minimise their own losses and take advantage of the fact that the enemy had not yet consolidated his equipment, to destroy his beachhead 'at one blow'. While defence in depth was now the favoured approach, the Japanese were still intent on stopping the Marines dead at the water's edge if they could – as any veteran of the battle can testify. The garrison was to 'recognise the limits of naval and aerial bombardments'; and to take advantage of the terrain 'according to necessity'. Tarawa and other battles had demonstrated that a surprisingly high proportion of defenders could expect to survive the apparently devastating naval and air bombardment of their positions. At Tarawa some of the palm-log and sand blockhouses had up to 7 feet of overhead protection, and others were built from reinforced concrete up to 16in thick.

The order finishes with the usual call for every man to 'die honourably' and, more significantly, 'to contribute to the opening of a new phase of the war'. This was presumably a hint of recognition that the 'old phase' had not worked, and that from now on the war would be one of attrition.

The Imperial Army was a unique blend of modern weapons and tactics with an almost medieval culture, and the mental attitude of the Japanese soldier was always a puzzle to the Allied forces in the Pacific and Asian theatre. The Japanese conscript was the product of a society that had been authoritarian and hierarchical since the earliest times. In every aspect of life the emphasis was placed not on the individual's rights, but on the absolute duty of conformity and obedience which he owed to the group and to his superiors. During the 1930s the militarist regime had saturated Japanese society with ultra-nationalist propaganda, playing to a centuries-old culture of chauvinist racism and to the cult of Emperor-worship. An overlapping network of social controls in community, school and workplace kept the individual under perpetual surveillance – and with the willing co-operation of the majority.

When a simple villager or city labourer was called up for military service, his family were encouraged to more or less give him up for dead – and proudly; his life was now at the disposal of the Divine Emperor. Military training was thorough and fiercely disciplined, and unquestioning obedience was enforced by physical brutality at every level. In the China campaigns it was not unusual for newly arrived replacements and junior officers to be required to kill a bound Chinese prisoner with the bayonet or the sword, to prove their hardihood. Contemptuous of the soft, undisciplined and arrogant Western democracies, Japanese soldiers were prepared to fight to the death as the proudest service that they could render the Emperor, thus ensuring that they joined the nation's guardian spirits memorialised at the Yasukuni shrine. They were genuinely at a loss to understand an enemy who allowed himself to be taken prisoner; their national tradition revered not only warriors who died in battle, but also those who took their own lives in the name of honour. While this culture cannot excuse their always callous, and sometimes bestial treatment of civilians and Allied prisoners of war, it does go some way to explain it.

The other side of the coin was the cold hatred of the Japanese felt by most Allied front-line soldiers, who fully returned the enemy's racial contempt. The widespread stories of Japanese cruelty towards Allied prisoners and wounded, many of them solidly founded in fact, aroused a mixture of fear and determination to show no mercy in return. Grim experience had taught that even an apparently helpless enemy casualty might produce a grenade and try to 'take one with him'. No Marine was going to take that chance; if the Japanese soldier was determined to fight to the death, then no American was going to risk his own life to frustrate that wish. Infantry fighting in Europe was a lot more merciless than post-war movies made out; but even so, American, British and German soldiers basically recognised their opponents as sharing a common humanity. This recognition was largely absent from the Pacific battlefields, on both sides of the lines.

* * *

Colonel Nakagawa had sited artillery in the Umurbrogol – some of the guns were even mounted on tracks and concealed behind steel doors. Mortars in camouflaged pits had the beaches, and the vital shallows on the reef, bracketed to the nearest yard. Ditches to trap tanks were dug parallel to the landing beaches, bunkers housing machine guns covered all access to the airfield, and the approaches to these positions were linked and covered by open fire trenches. All wartime Allied intelligence appreciations stress the excellence of Japanese field engineering; their fighting positions were skilfully sited to deliver interlocking fields of fire in mutual support, solidly protected, and superbly concealed and camouflaged.

Nakagawa's principal advantage lay in the terrain of the island. Peleliu is approximately 6 miles long and 2 miles wide at its extremities, and is completely surrounded by reefs. The airfield site was the only area of continuous flat ground in the south; the landing beaches were immediately to the west, and to the east the airfield was effectively isolated by a large inlet of mangrove swamp. Peleliu's most striking feature, as we have seen, was the Umurbrogol area of wooded high ground immediately to the north-west of the airfield, which sloped away northwards towards the tip of the island, where more woods and hills overlooked the causeway to the nearby island of Ngesebus.

The massive bombardment prior to the US landings would strip the lush foliage from the Umurbrogol, revealing its true nature as a chaotic labyrinth of small valleys, cliffs, coral outcrops and walls, liberally dotted with natural and man-made caves (whose entrances and gun-slits the fallen foliage would help to conceal from troops advancing on the ground). The Japanese caves on Peleliu were probably only surpassed in scope and complexity by those prepared by Gen. Kuribayashi on Iwo Jima some five months later. Construction had been started nearly a year earlier by the 214th Naval Construction Battalion, and their size and extent were to astonish the Marines who would spend many weeks prising out the fanatical defenders. These were not merely rocky bolt-holes from which a few men with a machine gun could sell their lives dearly. The larger cave systems contained air-raid shelters, living areas, hospitals, supply dumps and cooking facilities; galleries extended into the hills for hundreds of yards, with multiple entrances and exits. A full five months after the end of the battle, five enemy soldiers were still shooting at the Americans from one of these strongholds.

The Japanese suffered a chronic shortage of land mines, and were forced to improvise by using aircraft bombs fitted with crude detonating horns. These were largely ineffectual, since the horns could easily be seen, and many failed to explode because of inefficient fuzes. The US Navy were more concerned about the possibility of underwater obstacles on the landing beaches, a problem they had already encountered in the Marianas. Aerial reconnaissance and photographs taken by US submarines lying off shore had convinced them that the enemy were building underwater obstructions; consequently, men of the Navy's Underwater Demolition Teams (UDTs) were tasked to deal with the problem. Variously known as the 'naked warriors', 'mermen', or 'half-fish, half-nuts', these remarkably brave volunteers – working with little more than fins and masks, in those days long before the invention of SCUBA gear – had already proved their worth by clearing beaches as far afield as North Africa, Normandy and Saipan.

Boarding the submarine *Burrfish* in July, UDT swimmers had reconnoitred the beaches of Peleliu and Angaur despite heavy opposition from the enemy, who had picked up their boats on radar. Two days before the September invasion landing craft dropped the men of Teams 6 and 7 at low tide, and they immediately came under fire from enemy snipers and machine guns. Covering the northern sector (White Beaches 1 & 2), Team 7 found a blockade of tetrahedrons, steel pyramids and wooden posts which they estimated would take a full day to clear. On the southern beaches (Orange Beaches 1, 2 & 3), Team 6 also located tetrahedrons and coconut-palm logs strung with barbed wire. Both teams accomplished their highly dangerous tasks. Team 6 blew two wide channels for Tank Landing Ships and DUKWs on the southern beaches – most of the time under enemy fire. On White 1 & 2, two ten-man squads of Team 7 blasted similar paths through the tetrahedrons. Their work continued even after D-Day; on D+3 men of Team 7 cleared minefields that had been laid during the previous night by the Japanese, and Team 6 personnel blew up 300 yards of concrete, wooden posts and steel tripods close to the front line.

On Angaur the three proposed invasion beaches were surveyed by Team 8. The only obstacles that they found were some 50 steel rails wedged into the coral near the waterline on the northern beach; these were either blown up or, in some cases, manhandled out of the way. When the 81st Division made their landing on Angaur on 17 September, men of the UDTs guided the waves of tanks, landing craft and DUKWs ashore, only interrupting their work briefly when a school of sharks approached the beaches. The contribution made by this little-known branch of the Navy to the overall success of the operation is difficult to assess, but it is certain that the Marines who formed the vanguard of the assault on D-Day had reason to be more than grateful for their outstanding work.

* * *

In early September the first Marines left Pavuvu: 30 LSTs plodding along at their best speed of 7.7 knots, carrying the assault companies and their Amtracs. On 8 September 17 troop transport ships departed with the remainder of the division, scheduled to join up before the convoy reached the Palaus.

One battalion commander recalls his personal unease as the convoy departed. Shortly before leaving, Gen. Rupertus had called a meeting of his line commanders and staff, among them the divisional artillery commander, chief of staff, and the assistant divisional commander, Oliver Smith. He told them: 'You have your orders. I will not be ashore on D-Day and may not be there on D+l, it depends on the course of the action. But I want you to understand now that there will be no change in orders regardless. Even if General Smith attempts to change my plans or orders, you Regimental Commanders will refuse to obey.'

This astonishing statement – openly undermining the authority of the second-in-command, and disregarding the inevitable need to adjust prior orders according to the developing shape of any battle – must have been not only deeply embarrassing for Smith, but seriously worrying for the division's senior officers.

The course of the convoy took them north-west, weaving through the Solomon Islands, across the Equator and along the coast of New Guinea – some 2,100 miles in all. The weather was kind, but the crowded conditions, particularly aboard the LSTs where most of the Marines were compelled to sleep on the deck, made the trip very uncomfortable. 'As I write, I realize that this may be my last letter. I, too, am without illusions, but my love for you keeps me at peace', wrote Jim Johnston to his parents as he headed for the shores of Peleliu.

* * *

Three days before the invasion, on 12 September, the Fire Support Group commanded by Rear Adm. Jesse Oldendorf began their bombardment of Peleliu. Lying some 7,500 yards offshore and spread over 12 miles of ocean, the flotilla which the US Navy could devote to the invasion of this speck of coral was awesomely powerful.

Surrounded by a swarm of destroyers to guard them from submarine or air attack were the battleships USS *Tennessee, Idaho, Maryland, Mississippi* and *Pennsylvania.* Most of the battleships were 'old ladies' – three had been repaired after suffering serious damage at Pearl Harbor. All were relatively slow and semi-obsolete, unable to keep up with the Fast Attack Carrier Groups now roaming the Pacific; but they still packed a devastating weight of metal and explosive with their multiple 16in and 14in gun turrets. Supporting the battleships were the heavy cruisers *Minneapolis, Indianapolis, Louisville, Portland* and *Columbus*, with 8in guns, and the light cruisers *Denver, Cleveland* and *Honolulu*, whose turrets housed 5in and 6in guns.

The planners had allowed three days for the Navy to soften up the island. Now, in the pre-dawn darkness, the roar of the huge guns seemed to split the sky. A broadside by heavy naval guns – nine or 12 in each of the battleships, firing shells which weighed as much as a small car – was probably the most stunning demonstration of destructive power seen in the Second World War. To the men on board the great orange flashes seemed to light up the sea from horizon to horizon; to men below their path, the shells made a sound which was often described as like a passing express train. Massive explosions flung up clouds of dirt and smoke as the fall of the shells churned across the beaches of Peleliu and moved inland to the airfield and the foothills overlooking it.

As the sun began to rise at 6.00am, the firing abruptly ceased. Below the horizon, 15 miles off shore, lay the air support for the invasion – no fewer than three fleet and five escort carriers, their hangars and decks crammed with more than 400 aircraft. Now, as a stunned silence fell over the shell-ravaged island, wave after wave of blunt-nosed, dark blue Navy fighters and bombers came buzzing overhead, making low-level passes to drop 500lb bombs and napalm canisters before circling back to strafe 'targets of opportunity' until their ammunition was exhausted.

As the planes headed back for the carriers, the battleships renewed their pounding; and so it continued until nightfall on 12 September – thunderclaps of naval gunfire interlaced with aerial attacks. Just before dark a reconnaissance aircraft slowly made a low-level flight over the whole of southern Peleliu, photographing the results of the day's hammering. The wet prints were rushed to Adm. Oldendorf and his staff aboard his flagship, the USS *Pennsylvania*. They showed that virtually all ground-level fortifications appeared to have been destroyed. The airfield runways and hangars were in an even worse state than they had been immediately after the attentions of Task Force 58 in March, and the nearby barracks area had been reduced to ruins.

As daylight broke on 13 September, many eyes on many ships scanned the island through powerful binoculars. Some were amazed at the transformation that had taken place. Gone was the lush foliage that had previously carpeted the Umurbrogol and its foothills; in its place, like a jumble of bones, there stood revealed the maze of cliffs and gulches that was to be the graveyard of hundreds of Marines and soldiers in the coming weeks.

Now began another day of intense naval gunfire and carrier air raids which continued until dusk, when Oldendorf gathered his staff to discuss progress. The admiral stated that he could see no point in carrying on with the proposed third day of the bombardment, and radioed to Adm. Nimitz at Pearl Harbor that he had 'run out of targets'.

General Holland Smith, the Marine supremo in the Pacific, was scathing in his criticism of this and most other pre-invasion bombardments carried out by the Navy. In his post-war memoirs, '*Coral and Brass*', he slammed the contribution of the Fire Support Groups at Tarawa, the Marianas, Peleliu and Iwo Jima as being inadequate and ineffectual – a charge vigorously denied by the US Navy. While Holland Smith's views were doubtless contentiously expressed, there can be no doubt that the decision to grant the defenders of Peleliu 24 hours to recover from the bombardment before facing the landings was a fundamental, indeed an inexplicable error. What Gens Geiger and Rupertus thought is not known; both were on their way to Peleliu under a radio blackout. But there can be no doubt that Gen. Inoue and Col. Nakagawa were delighted as 14 September wore on, and they slowly realised that they had a full day's respite to repair what they could and re-sight their guns and mortars.

A Japanese submarine had earlier reported that a heavily escorted convoy of troopships sailing south off the Palaus had now swung north; Gen. Inoue was in no doubt as to where it was heading.

CHAPTER 6

One Day in Hell

On 15 September 1944 the day dawned slightly overcast but dry, with good visibility and only a slight swell on the sea. Before the sun was up Adm. Oldendorf's battlewagons were once again pounding the shoreline with their massive shells, and by full daylight most of the western side of Peleliu lay under a huge grey-brown pall of smoke and dust.

On the command ship *Mount McKinley* which housed the communications centre for the operation, Rear Adm. George Fort, Maj.Gen. Julian Smith and Maj.Gen. Roy Geiger anxiously scanned the island through their binoculars, as wave upon wave of carrier planes dipped and rose through the smoke, bombing and machine-gunning the shoreline for the last time before the presence of Marines on the beaches complicated their missions. On the 1st Division's floating headquarters, the troop transport *DuPage*, an optimistic Gen. Rupertus was enthroned in a deckchair with his leg in plaster. Aboard the transport *Elmore*, Brig.Gen. Oliver Smith was preparing for his embarkation; as the first general officer to go ashore, he was anxious to establish his command post as soon as practicable.

Colonel 'Chesty' Puller, commander of the 1st Marine Regiment, also gazed anxiously towards the beaches. 'You won't find anything to stop you over there – nothing could have lived through that hammering', said the skipper of his ship. Puller was not reassured.

The goal was to get 4,500 men ashore in 19 minutes – a formidable task that required exhaustive and intricate planning, split-second timing, and a good deal of luck. Mounting an amphibious operation demanded skill and organisation on a monumental scale. The warships and transports had to be in position on time; the unloading of the troops onto their Amtracs and bobbing, box-like 'Higgins' landing craft needed to be worked out to the minute; all craft had to be lined up off shore in a pre-planned sequence; naval gunfire and air attacks had to be worked out to the second so as to coincide with but not endanger the landings. Once a beachhead had been secured, the follow-up flow of reinforcements, supplies, ammunition, and the thousands of items needed daily by the troops in the field would have to continue for weeks – regardless of weather and enemy retaliation.

A legacy of the Marine Corps' rest periods in Australia and New Zealand was the steak-and-egg breakfast, and this had now become the traditional meal served up on the troop transports before each invasion. Not all the troops were in the mood for such greasy fare; with fear gnawing at their stomachs, the very thought was enough to make many vomit. (This treat was also frowned upon by the Navy doctors, who were aware that they would certainly be treating many abdominal wounds before the day was out.) On the other hand, veterans of previous landings knew only too well that this might be their last square meal for days – perhaps even weeks.

Shortly before 8.00am, and masked behind a screen of white smoke shells, 18 Landing Craft Infantry (LCIs) equipped with banks of 4.5in rockets approached the landing beaches and plastered the shoreline. Behind them, precisely at 8.00am, the first assault waves crossed the 'line of departure'. Up front were the Landing Vehicles Tracked (Armored) – LVT(A)s – of the 3rd Armored Amphibian Tractor Battalion. These 'Amtanks' were Amtracs with an armoured superstructure mounting a tank turret equipped with either a 37mm or a snub-nosed 75mm gun; they were the vanguard, scheduled to drive straight across the reef some 700–800 yards from the shore, and clear the beaches for the first waves of Marines following up in their LVTs.

Most of these troop- and cargo-carrying Amtracs of the 1st and 8th Amphibian Tractor Battalions were open-topped amphibious vehicles, propelled both at sea and on land by their special caterpillar tracks. Their value was that this unique method of propulsion allowed them – unlike the landing craft, which were true boats – to crawl across the reefs which guarded Pacific coastlines, and carry up to 20 men right onto the beach. Only lightly armoured around the cab and armed with a couple of machine guns, the LVTs were highly vulnerable to enemy fire, and the Marines could only disembark from them by scrambling over the high sides. The latest LVT-4 Amtracs had loading ramps that dropped from the rear, providing safer disembarkation; but only about 50 of these had arrived at the last minute, to be hastily formed into a provisional 6th Battalion with only partly trained crews.

The configuration of the reef off south-west Peleliu had forced the planners to adopt a complex system for getting most of the Marines ashore – and the more complex a plan, the more things can go wrong. The first assault wave of Amtanks and Amtracs would be launched by the Landing Ships Tank (LSTs) a safe distance from the reef, and would ride straight in. But the ocean-going transport ships carrying the rest of the division had to stay 18,000 yards off shore, out of possible enemy artillery range; and the wallowing Amtracs could not be launched safely that far from land. Their troops would therefore have to embark first into Landing Craft Vehicle/Personnel (LCVPs), which would take them to a 'transfer line' at the edge of the reef. There they would have to clamber from the awkward 'Higgins boats' into Amtracs, which would run a shuttle service between the reef and beach. Once the Marines were on the beaches, the waterproofed Sherman tanks of the 1st Tank Battalion would leave the LCTs and cross the half-mile from the edge of the reef under their own power, to provide much-needed close gunfire support.

In the event, what happened was not exactly what the planners had envisaged. The 'landing luck' of the Old Breed ran out at Peleliu.

* * *

'Early that morning I had gone through the usual gut-wrenching trip over the side of the transport and down the cargo net into the little landing craft', remembers Jim Johnston of the 5th Marines. 'Beside the helmet and the clothing that I wore, I carried the following gear: backpack with entrenching tool, one poncho, three light and three heavy rations, two packs of cigarettes in a waxed paper sack, a small leather case fitted with weapons cleaning gear, one extra pair of socks, one gas mask, one cartridge belt, one personal sidearm [.45in pistol] with two extra ammunition clips, one sterile canned compress [wound dressing], two canteens of water, one GI knife, two fragmentation grenades, and one Browning light machine gun, Model 1919A4 (weight 36lbs). I carried two additional objects the Corps would have confiscated if they had known about them: a pair of binoculars that I had picked up on New Britain, and a Smith & Wesson .38 Special [revolver] that I had traded with a Navy pilot for a good Japanese flag.'

Tom Lea, an artist and correspondent for *Time/Life* magazine, was also contemplating his trip ashore. Correspondents were not as thick on the ground at Peleliu as they had been during previous Marine landings – which is the reason usually given for the poor coverage of the battle and the subsequent obscurity of the operation. General Rupertus had announced at his briefing that it would all be over in a matter of days, so the majority of the press decided that they would give Peleliu a miss and head for the Marianas to wait for the coming assault on Iwo Jima. The absurdity of the general's prediction coupled with the heavy casualties that the division actually suffered probably encouraged the Corps to allow press attention to be diverted elsewhere. (In the event, Peleliu would provide Tom Lea with an image which has become known far beyond the context of the Pacific War: the painting now known as *'The Two-Thousand Yard Stare'*, but which he originally captioned 'Down from Bloody Nose Ridge too late, he's finished, washed up – gone').

Along with Lea, one other well-known correspondent who was staring at the smoke pall hanging over Peleliu that morning was Joe Rosenthal of Associated Press. Small and slightly myopic, Rosenthal was an unlikely figure to be found among the chaos of the battlefield, but he already had an enviable reputation for getting into the thick of the action. Rosenthal had no idea now – and nor would he until after it had been printed – that some five months later he would achieve world fame with what was to become the most famous photograph of the entire war: his superb shot of the flag-raising on the summit of Mount Suribachi on Iwo Jima.

Although strictly Navy personnel, the 'Corpsmen' – the medical orderlies who accompanied the Marines on all operations – were held in the highest respect by the Leathernecks. Throughout the war Corpsmen performed acts of outstanding bravery while tending to wounded Marines in the front line, and were awarded a total of seven Medals of Honor.

At 33, Brooking Rouse Gex was an old man compared to the average Marine at Peleliu: 'I had been trained as a hospital Corpsman. My job was to bandage wounded troops under fire on the front line, to keep injured men alive until we could get them to the Navy hospital ships anchored offshore where surgeons awaited. On this day in mid-September, as one of the several Pharmacist's Mates, I was poised at the ship's rail ready to land with the Marines; it was my constant fear that I'd get wounded and not be able to care for the men.'

* * *

As the first waves of Amtanks and Amtracs approached the pale blue water marking the reef, the huge cloud of smoke and dust raised by the barrage from the warships and the salvos of rockets from the LCIs began slowly to settle and drift seawards, obscuring the shoreline under a heavy veil. Riding low in the water, the spaced-out lines of Navy-grey amphibians passed into its shadow, and disappeared. For what seemed like an age the dust and smoke hung over the coast of Peleliu; and when it finally dissipated in the gentle breeze, it revealed a scene that shocked the onlookers on the ships off shore. All along the reef, columns of black oily smoke rose from blazing Amtracs and DUKWs.

When the Navy barrage lifted to targets inland, the Japanese had emerged from their shelters. With ranges long pre-registered to the nearest yard, the artillery and mortars had laid a barrage all along the White and Orange beaches, and within ten minutes 26 Amtracs were reduced to blazing wrecks.

On the cruiser *Portland* a sharp-eyed gunnery officer trained his binoculars on a ridge north of the airfield, and saw a door open at the entrance of a large cave. An artillery piece emerged, fired at the beach, then disappeared as the steel door closed again. The *Portland* fired five 8in shells at the position, but between salvos the gun emerged unscathed and continued to pound the beaches. 'You could put all the steel in Pittsburgh onto that thing and still not get it', the officer declared in disgust. Jesse Oldendorf's claim to have 'run out of targets' was beginning to sound a little hollow that morning.

* * *

Offshore the Marines continued to embark. Corpsman Brooking Gex vividly recalls his departure:

'"OK, Doc", said a loud voice – "Let's go". I scrambled over the rail and onto the netting that formed a ladder down the side of the ship; amphibious tractors waited below. I was 33 years old, 5ft 9ins, 150lbs, but not the most agile sailor to participate in the landing, particularly with 120lbs of medical supplies on my back. When the ship rolled my foot missed the netting and I fell down towards the sea, then I felt myself being pulled up short – a hardened Marine had grabbed my pack in mid-air. He held me until the ship rolled back and I was able to regain my footing and hurry down.

'Our Amtrac steered a zig-zag course towards the beach under the thunder of enemy fire; the noise deafened us, geysers of seawater erupted everywhere as the enemy shelling intensified. The vessel beside us was hit while I watched helplessly – its occupants never reached the beach. Bodies floated around us, the water surged with explosions and the air was thick with the screams of the wounded and the dying – half of our troops were killed on the way to shore. Amazed to be still alive, I joined a patrol party on the beach, [whose] own Corpsman had been killed; 48 of us crawled from tree to tree, hiding among the bushes to assess the situation – after one hour our patrol was reduced to eight.'

At the reef the situation was becoming chaotic. Marines who had made the first lift towards the shore in Higgins boats were waiting for Amtracs to shuttle them in, but these were becoming fewer and fewer. Correspondent Tom Lea's boat wallowed just short of the reef about 100 yards ahead: 'The first Jap mortar burst hit just inside the reef as our coxswain worked us up alongside an LVT for transfer; as the two craft bobbed and smashed at each other, we put ourselves and our gear into the LVT, the coxswain of the LCVP waved, backed his craft clear and headed seaward.'

Despite the heavy casualties, the troops continued to embark for the beaches. Many would recall the fear and the tension that seized them even before leaving the LSTs. They were herded into their Amtracs in the dark bowels of the landing ships, their eyes streaming from the diesel fumes; a cheer would sound as the chains rattled and the bow slapped into the sea, the Amtrac would surge forward and then down into the water as men grabbed something or someone in their effort to stay upright. Finally, blinded by the daylight and gulping in the fresh air, they were on their way towards the shore which lay in the distance wreathed in smoke, while overhead the shells from the battleships roared past like locomotives.

* * *

'Good luck, Puller – we'll expect you for dinner this evening', quipped a naval officer as the colonel made his way from the bridge to his transport. 'Chesty' was scheduled to go in on the third wave and he was in no mood for the Navy man's flippancy. His 1st Regiment had been assigned White Beaches 1 & 2 on the extreme left of the landing zone, and so far things were running to schedule; the first of his men were on the beach and they were only two minutes late. The 2/1st Marines were to land on the right (White 2), and the 3/1st on the left (White 1); the 1st Battalion were in reserve, scheduled to land at 9.45am. As the enemy's barrage of artillery and mortar fire intensified, some of the first landing craft to be hit were those carrying the 1st Regiment's radio equipment – a severe blow that was to result in a serious breakdown in communications at an early stage of the battle.

Despite the availability of the LVT(A)-1 and -4 Amtanks of the Armored Amphibian Tractor Battalions, the Marine Corps remained convinced that the Shermans of their divisional Tank Battalions needed to get on shore as early as possible in an opposed landing. The Amtank was not a true combat vehicle, but an improvised stop-gap built on the unarmoured chassis of a flimsy cargo-carrier – better than nothing, but not to be relied upon. A marked feature of the Peleliu operation was the rapid deployment of the Shermans in support of the initial landing force.

The Underwater Demolition Teams had done an excellent job in clearing the worst of the obstacles, and 18 waterproofed Shermans of the 1st Tank Battalion began to wade forward across the reef off the White Beaches in support of Puller's 1st Marines. However, such was the accuracy and intensity of the enemy fire that only one tank arrived on the beach undamaged. Fortunately the water acted as a cushion, and only three of the disabled tanks were knocked out completely; the others were still able to fire their main armament, acting as off-shore pillboxes to add useful support for the infantry.

All along the reef, Higgins boats bobbed around at the edge of the shallows waiting for Amtracs to take their loads of Marines to the beaches. As the number of waiting landing craft increased, and the number of Amtracs returning to the reef became fewer, Japanese fire was taking a fearful toll. Flaming wrecks were everywhere; bodies and parts of bodies bobbed grotesquely in the pink-stained water; and a surreal touch was added by a nearby LST, from whose loudspeakers the Marine Corps hymn blared out – '*From the Halls of Montezuma, to the shores of Tripoli . . .* '. The music faded as another Amtrac received a direct hit; blazing fuel spread over the water as men leaped out of the twisted wreckage.

* * *

At the southern end of the beach, on Orange 3, Col. Hanneken's 7th Regiment were making their landing amid a ferocious barrage. Tom Lea was among the early arrivals, and recalls the scene:

'We ground to a stop, after a thousand years, on the coarse coral; the ramp aft – seaward – cranked down fast, and we tightened our hold on our gear. The air cracked and roared, filling our ears and guts with its sound while Farrell bellowed, "OK! Pile out! Scatter – but follow me to the right – the right, Goddammit, remember!"

'And we ran down the ramp and came around the end of the LVT, splashing ankle deep up the surf to the white beach, then I ran to the right – slanting up the beach for cover, half bent over, off balance.

'I fell flat on my face just as I heard the *whishhh* of a mortar I knew was too close, a red flash stabbed at my eyeballs. About fifteen yards [away], on the upper edge of the beach, it smashed down four men from our boat; one figure seemed to fly to pieces, with terrible clarity I saw the head and one leg sail in the air. Captain Farrell, near the burst, never dodged or hesitated but kept running, screaming at his men to follow him to their objective down the beach.

'I got up to follow him, ran a few steps, and fell into a small shell hole as another mortar threw dirt on me. Lying there in terror, I saw a wounded man near me, staggering in the direction of the LVTs, his face was half bloody pulp and the mangled shreds of what was left of an arm hung down like a stick as he bent over in his stumbling, shock-crazed walk. The half of his face that was still human had the most terrible look of abject patience I have ever seen. He fell behind me in a red puddle on the white sand.'

Orange Beach 3 was the narrowest of the five invasion beaches, roughly 500 yards north to south, and this resulted in the two battalions of the 7th Marines having to land in column of battalions – one behind the other. As the Amtracs approached the beach they came under very heavy fire from enemy positions to their right on a small unnamed island a few yards offshore, and on a wooded promontory sometimes called Ngarmoked Island (although it was strictly part of the mainland). This fire caused many of the coxswains to veer off to their left in an attempt to escape the pounding, and resulted in some 7th Regiment units becoming intermixed with the 5th Marines on Orange Beach 2.

The lead battalion, the 3/7th, were to drive straight across the island to the eastern swamp supported by the 5th Marines on their left flank; the 1/7th, landing immediately behind them, were to swing to the right to attack the enemy, who would hopefully be cut off. In their efforts to impede the Marines the Japanese had inadvertently provided them with a useful mustering point. They had dug a tank trap which ran parallel to the beach, stretching the full length of Orange 3. As the Marines ran for cover the anti-tank ditch provided a temporary refuge in which to rest and re-organise before pushing forward to their objectives. Major E.Hunter

Hurst, commanding officer of the 3/7th, recorded in the official USMC history of the battle:

'Once officers were able to orient themselves in the anti-tank ditch it proved an excellent artery for moving troops into the proper position for deployment and advance inland, since it crossed the entire width of our zone of action approximately parallel to the beach. With respect to the Battalion Command Post, I am convinced that it enabled us to join the two principal echelons of Command Post personnel and commence functioning as a complete unit at least an hour earlier than otherwise would have been possible. After announcing our locations to each other, it was simply a question of jumping in the ditch, meeting in the middle, and jumping out again to displace farther inland.'

* * *

'Soon we were churning towards the beach', said Jeb Lord, a seventeen-year old from the 7th Regiment's 1st Battalion. 'I was amazed at the amount of fire being poured into the island from the ships and planes. I don't remember being afraid as we landed, I was more excited than anything, I suppose. I remember watching a Marine walk up to a dug-out entrance and throw in a grenade, he just stood there until it exploded and some of the shrapnel flew out and hit him. He was evacuated – I wondered if he got the Purple Heart; if they gave out "stupid medals" he would have gotten one.'

Amtracs continued to arrive on Orange Beach 3 despite the accurate and withering fire, particularly from the right flank. In one of them was Pte. Charles Owen of the 1st Battalion's Company A. At sixteen years of age Owen was something of a veteran, having lied his way into the Corps at the tender age of fourteen. He recalls:

'Although I and fellow Marines had been instructed repeatedly in our training exercises that the beach was the last place we would want to be, in the face of fire from our front and the converging fire to our right and left, all of which was sweeping through the ranks of us on the beach with the most terrible and fearful effect, I and those of my company around me remained frozen to the beach with fear. I was literally terrified, and the first thing that I saw that had an effect on my mind was either an arm or a leg that fell down beside me.'

As Owen tried to remember exactly why it was that he had gone to such trouble to enlist, and why he had requested combat duty after being offered an easy posting on a training ship tied up in the Norfolk Navy Yard, a voice – a very loud voice, that could be heard even above the roar of battle – interrupted his reverie.

'I looked about me, [but] there was nobody in our immediate area. I looked again, down to my right, and at a point on the beach where the storm was raging most furiously, there was a man coming up the beach towards us – he was the only person on his feet as far as I could see. While the enemy artillery, machine gun and small arms fire seemed to be at its height, it was startling to see a man unflinchingly walk in our direction and ignore it completely. It still rings in my ears today as he screamed, "Get the hell off this beach, or I'll shoot your ass!"

'He was raising hell with those of us on that beach. As he got closer I noticed that he was a major; he was armed with a Tommy gun, had a Jap shovel across one shoulder, was bloodied and mud-encrusted and was kicking and screaming, and just before he got to me, all I could think of was this crazy sonofabitch is going to kill me if I don't get the hell off this beach. With that I ignored everything else, all of the incoming fire, and I got to hell off that beach – which undoubtedly saved my life, for I learned later that a tremendous mortar barrage came down right where a moment before we had been lying.'

For many years Owen, who went on to serve in Okinawa, Korea and Vietnam before retiring from the Corps in 1962, wondered who that major was, and if he had survived Peleliu. He was finally to find out 48 years later when, through the 1st Marine Division Association, he was to meet up again with the man who saved his life that day – Major Arthur Middleton Parker Jr (a direct descendant of Arthur Middleton, who as a member of Congress signed the engrossed copy of the Declaration of Independence on 2 August 1776). Owen immediately recognised the booming voice, and learned for the first time about the events leading up to their encounter.

Major Parker had been the executive officer of the 3rd Armored Amphibian Tractor Battalion, in one of the 73 Amtanks moving in lines abreast for the assault. When his tank was about 500 yards from the beach it hit a coral head and stopped dead in the water. Acting against orders, Lt. Bristol, the commanding officer of Company D, pulled out of line and connected a tow cable to Parker's tank. He dragged it clear, but under heavy fire the major's tank was hit twice and disabled, one of the crew being killed.

Taking to the beach, Parker saw that there was a conglomeration of infantry all in one place, a certain target for the Japanese artillery and mortars: 'Although I had nothing to do with these infantrymen, other than to help them, they had to be gotten off that beach or they would all be killed. They seemed to be paralysed with fear, they wouldn't move, so I screamed at them, I used all kinds of profanities – I had a Tommy gun slung on my arm . . . and blood and mud all over me – I must have been a horrible sight to behold.'

Once the Marines had moved off the beach, Maj. Parker went about the task of mustering his decimated battalion; he commandeered an Amtank and again took command. Lieutenant Bristol got his tank onto the beach, but then it took a hit and had to be abandoned. The lieutenant had forgotten to collect his Thompson gun and went back for it; as he climbed into the turret a mortar bomb made a direct hit and blew him to pieces.

* * *

Operation Plan 1-44 for Maj. Parker's battalion had included the following simple 'mission statement':

'Precede LVTs in accordance with Landing Plan en route to Beaches White 1 & 2 and Orange 1, 2 & 3, landing at How-Hour [0830, 15 September]. Neutralise shore defences by fire with particular attention to flanks. After passing through the water line beach defences . . . render immediate fire support for assault waves.'

The 3rd Armored Tractors had been the first Marines ashore on D-Day. Sergeant Albert Blaisdell of 'Baker' Company Headquarters remembers the awesome noise and clouds of smoke, the Navy Hellcats and Dauntlesses pounding the beach area, dust, flames, debris, bits of trees being hurled into the air:

'As the shelling lifted off the beach and moved inland, we reached the coral reef and began climbing over very rough coral. Our tracks churned up salt water and sand, we were worried about mines and unexploded shells (ours), as we could not see under the surface of the water at all. Looking back seaward, I could see all of our landing craft (infantry) lined up abreast and following us. Shells began hitting among them, and soon machine gun bursts began to hit the water around us; we began firing back with our machine guns and the 75s began firing at targets.'

It was easy to tell which of the battalion's Amtanks were commanded by officers – you just had to count the number of radio antennae. Each LVT(A) had one radio with one antenna; but company commanders had two, because they needed to talk to the battalion staff; and the battalion commander (Lt.Col. Kimber H.Boyer) and the battalion executive officer (Maj. Parker) had five antennae, to enable them to speak to each company.

At around 10.30am Lt.Col. Boyer had established his command post just inland from Orange 1, and began to contact his sub-units which were scattered along the full length of the invasion beaches. The news was not encouraging: casualties had been higher than he had anticipated, and the smoking wreckage on White 1 and Orange 3 told its own story. Of the 73 vehicles which had been launched to assault the beaches only 45 were still operational; two officers had been killed, and of the enlisted men 26 were dead, 78 wounded and four missing.

Oliver Sweetland recalls that one of the most difficult things for him on

D-Day was trying to have a bowel movement; when achieved, the event stood out in his memory because it was the last one that he was to have for several days. Second Lieutenant Glen Blitgen comments: 'Ollie hasn't said a lot about his activities except, "just doing my job"; but I'm sure that he did a hell of a lot more than just have a bowel movement on D-Day!'

* * *

On Orange Beaches 1 & 2 in the centre, the 1/5th and 3/5th Marines (respectively) encountered slightly less resistance than the 1st and 7th Regiments – the anti-boat fire which was proving so lethal against the landing craft on both flanks was not as effective here, and the ground to their front was less heavily defended.

As the terrain was more favourable for manoeuvre, the 1st Battalion were able to push forward to the airfield; but there they were forced to stop, partly because of the inability of the 1st Marines from White 2 to link up with them on their left, and partly because of the vicious mortar and artillery fire raining down on them from the foothills of the Umurbrogol to the north. Jim Johnston got ashore directly west of the airfield about an hour after the first wave:

'When we reached the shore and disembarked, I saw one hell of a sight up and down the beach. The sand was already littered with dead and mutilated bodies of US Marines – bodies of old salts and new selective service recruits lying side by side, you couldn't tell one from the other. All the armored amphibs I could see had been knocked out and were burning. We went into the attack immediately. When we reached the cover of the brush strip we stopped; everywhere people were trying to figure out where everyone was (both our elements and theirs), and what the hell was going on. When the sun had come up that fateful morning the island looked like a burned matchhead or a clinker left in an old coal furnace; one of the odd things I remember is the mat of twigs that lay thick on the ground almost everywhere – shellfire hadn't blown them away – [they were] about the size of a person's little finger.'

The 1/5th, under Lt.Col. Robert Boyd, were on the western perimeter of the airfield within 30 minutes of landing, and began digging in. In addition to their machine guns and bazookas, four 37mm anti-tank guns from the 5th's regimental weapons company had been hauled forward, and three Shermans from Company B of the 1st Tank Battalion took up positions slightly to the rear of the riflemen. On their right, the 3/5th led by Lt.Col. Austin Shofner had reached the edge of the main runway. Here they awaited developments, under heavy fire from the high ground to the north, and hampered by the loss of much of the battalion's field telephone equipment on the way in.

It was during these early encounters with the defenders that Peleliu's first Medal of Honor was won. Lewis K.Bausell, a 20-year-old corporal with the 5th Regiment's 1st Battalion, was with a squad attacking pillboxes in the scrubland a little distance inland from the beach. Nearby, Lt. Jack Kimble and his men were using flamethrowers to flush out the enemy. Suddenly, a Japanese soldier rushed forward clutching a grenade to his body; it exploded blowing him to pieces. A second soldier soon followed and was immediately shot dead; but a third threw a grenade among Bausell's squad. There was nowhere for anyone to run or take cover, so Bausell dashed forward and threw himself onto the grenade, saving the lives of his comrades. Grievously wounded, he was evacuated to the hospital ship *Bountiful* but died shortly afterwards.

Over to the right on Orange 2 there was a good deal of confusion. Company K of the 3rd Battalion, 5th Marines were becoming mixed up with Company K of the 7th Marines, who had been forced to land on Orange 2 instead of Orange 3 by the volume of enemy fire from the vicinity of Ngarmoked Island. Sterling Mace was a rifleman with one of the confused Company Ks – that of the 3/5th Marines. He recalls the lines of LCIs blasting their salvos of rockets onto the beach, and the nervous cry of 'Slow down, you're going too fast!' as the Marines in his Amtrac discovered that they were about 15 yards in front of the main wave.

'There came the sound of grating sand and coral from the bottom of the tractor, the rear door drops down and we exit . . . as we're heading towards shore, a small dog is wagging its tail and barking at us; the sound is suddenly unheard as the tractor's gunner opens fire on the vegetation along the beach front – the last time we saw the dog the little guy was in a mad dash down the beach.'

* * *

By 9.35am, while the two identically named companies attempted to sort themselves out, the 5th's regimental reserve, its 2nd Battalion, had landed. A concerted move now got under way to advance eastwards across the island. The 3rd Battalion of the 5th had become disorganised after landing, and Lt.Col. Shofner's executive officer, Maj. Robert Ash, had been killed a few minutes after hitting the beach. Nevertheless the 3/5th pushed forward, and reduced many mutually supporting pillboxes and bunkers on the perimeter of the airfield.

The official history (see Hough, Select Bibliography) states: 'Considerable confusion exists as to what really happened to 3-5 during D-Day. The only extant official reports for 5 Regiment bearing on the subject are regimental war diaries and 3-5 record of operations, which do not agree on all points and frequently conflict with reports of the 7th

Regiment. This account supplements these basic sources with carefully screened material recently obtained from surviving officers who were on the scene; in view of the fallibility of the human memory five years after the event, allowance must be made for a certain amount of conjecture.'

Things were still hectic on the extreme right. The 7th Regiment had survived the enemy fire from Ngarmoked Island on the south-west promontory, but were hampered by mines and barbed wire on the beach. Some of these mines were of a peculiar design, with twin horns consisting of lead-covered bottles of acid which would detonate the explosives if broken; most of them were of poor construction, however, and fortunately failed to work. Other areas were strewn with aerial bombs which the enemy had substituted for mines; at least one Amtrac was seen to blow up after falling foul of one of these devices.

The anti-tank ditch situated a short way inland from the top of Orange 3 allowed the regiment to orient themselves before moving out, and progress became swift; by mid-morning they had advanced about 500 yards from the beach.

* * *

Brigadier-General Oliver Smith was itching to get ashore. Leaving the *Elmore* about 90 minutes after the first wave had touched down, he hailed an Amtrac and directed the driver to take him to Orange Beach 2. On the approach the driver throttled his engine and ran full tilt into the reef, sending everyone, including the general, sprawling; he then turned north and followed a barbed wire fence running parallel to the beach. 'Look, you're going to run out of beach here pretty quickly, and we've got to move in', shouted Smith; so the driver turned right and landed Smith and his party on the northern extremity of Orange 2.

Coloured tapes had already been laid to mark mines, and the group moved off the beach into an anti-tank ditch. Here they set up the command post and assembled the radio equipment. Smith was soon in touch with the CPs of the 5th and 7th Regiments, and with Gen. Rupertus aboard the *DuPage*; however, all attempts to contact Puller's 1st Marines failed.

If things had gone to plan, Gen. Rupertus should have gone ashore no later than four hours after Smith; the divisional commander's optimistic plan predicted that the whole of the southern end of Peleliu would be occupied by then. His chief of staff, Col. Selden, advised against leaving before he knew exactly what the situation was ashore. Rupertus agreed; however, he insisted on committing the 5th Regiment's reserve, the 2/5th – much to the puzzlement of Oliver Smith, and to the annoyance of the 5th's commander Col. Harris, who wondered where he was going to find room for them on the crowded beachhead.

* * *

It was little wonder that Gen. Smith was unable to contact 'Chesty' Puller, since the 1st Regiment's radio equipment had been destroyed when the five Amtracs carrying the command group had been shot to pieces crossing the reef.

On White Beach 2 the 2nd Battalion landed against what the official history describes as 'moderate resistance' – not a term that veterans would subscribe to – but within an hour they had advanced some 350 yards. Lieutenant R.Bruce Watkins of Company E of the 2/1st remembers his arrival:

'Lurching and groaning, the Amtrac reached the beach and ran inland approximately 75 feet to the first line of battered trees and bushes. The ramp did stick for one everlasting moment, and then we poured out both sides; we formed a line along the edge of the undergrowth, making contact with Lt. Meyer's 3rd Platoon on our right, and started forward. Behind us, Amtracs in later waves were burning, and mortars started to fall around us. The Japs had survived the pounding and were up and firing; casualties from mortar fragments were plentiful and the 1st Platoon lost about six men in the first 100 yards, [though we] still hadn't seen a Jap.

'Sprinting across a flat open stretch we received heavy machine gun fire from our left flank, the bullets whistling and ricocheting on the coral deck. It was then that I heard Cpl. Alick calling me, "Lieutenant, help me – I can't move". Acting on instinct, I sprinted back to where Alick lay in the open stretch; he was shot through the thumb and thigh, his leg broken. Hugging the ground as best I could, I scooped him up and ran the last 50 feet to the embankment, sliding down in awkward fashion.

'There I found Sgt. Stasiak on his back holding his stomach with blood all over himself; he asked me to check and see how bad it was. A bullet had torn through flesh and muscle clear across at hip height and it looked real bad – I told him it looked worse than it was, counting on his toughness to keep him going. [Later] I saw them both on stretchers ready to be evacuated.

'We tied up with the 3rd Platoon who had just lost their lieutenant, "GoGo" Meyer: typically out in front of his men, he refused help when hit, knowing that he was dying and not wanting to risk his men in a futile rescue attempt.'

* * *

On White Beach 1 it was a different story: here the 3/1st Marines were to encounter the fiercest resistance of the entire landing.

Directly to the front of White 1 lay a coral ridge about 30 feet high which was dotted with caves and gun emplacements. There was no reference to a strongpoint at this location on the maps that had been issued to the regiment, and the naval bombardment had barely made any impression. A steady stream of withering machine gun and small arms fire was being directed at the Marines as they moved off the beach; even the presence of three Sherman tanks was of little help, and they soon retired under a hail of artillery and mortar fire. The few men who survived long enough to reach a tank trap at the foot of the ridge were pinned down, facing certain death if they either attacked or withdrew. Captain George Hunt, commander of Company K of the 3rd Battalion, described this ridge as being of solid, jagged coral, a mass of sharp pinnacles and tremendous boulders, interspersed with pillboxes reinforced with steel and concrete; he commented on the fact that the naval guns had left it untouched.

Colonel Puller landed on White 1 with the third wave. The artillery and mortar fire was horrendous, and he sprinted the 25 yards across the beach in double time despite sharp pains in his leg from a piece of shrapnel still lodged there from Guadalcanal. Looking back to the water's edge he was appalled to see the Amtrac that he had just left vanish in a cloud of smoke as a salvo of shells slammed into it, most of the crew dying instantly.

The beach was a chaotic sight; everywhere there were burning Amtracs, abandoned equipment and debris, exploding shells and mortar bombs, and the figures of dead and dying Marines. At the extreme left of White 1, rising to a height of around 30 feet and protruding into the sea, was a coral and rock promontory which the maps designated the Point. Captain Hunt and Company K were soon to suffer for the Navy's failure to destroy this position as Col. Puller had requested. Housing a 47mm artillery piece and a number of machine guns and other small arms, the Point had been developed into a formidable bastion from which the Japanese were able to wreak havoc across the entire length of White Beach 1 and half of White Beach 2.

Although he was not fully aware of it at the time, Puller and his 1st Marines were in serious trouble. On White 1, Lt.Col. Steven Sabol's 3rd Battalion had only advanced about 100 yards before being pinned down at the foot of the ridge under withering crossfire from the dozens of enemy strongpoints directly to their front. George Hunt's Company K, just short of the Point, were attempting a head-on assault, with disastrous results – before they had advanced 50 yards a storm of machine gun and mortar fire cut them to pieces, and the survivors took refuge in a tank trap. In 40 minutes the 2nd and 3rd Platoons had lost almost 50 per cent of their men killed or wounded.

In near desperation Hunt committed his reserve, the 1st Platoon under

2nd Lt. Willis, who pushed to the east and attacked the enfilading Japanese bastion from the landward side.

In a bloody mêlée that lasted for two hours, the 1st Platoon gradually battled their way with hand grenades and small arms to the emplacement of the 47mm gun that was responsible for much of the carnage on the White beaches. Willis worked his way up to the bunker and lobbed a smoke grenade through the firing aperture; then he dodged to one side as Cpl. Anderson aimed a rifle grenade. His first shot bounced off the surrounding concrete, but the second hit the gun barrel and landed among a pile of 47mm ammunition. As flames and smoke erupted, three screaming Japanese soldiers burst out of the rear exit and were gunned down by waiting Marines.

By 10.30am Captain Hunt and his men had fought their way to the crest of the Point and established a defensive perimeter among the corpses of about a hundred Japanese defenders. The cost had been appalling: Hunt made a rough estimate that almost two-thirds of Company K were either dead or wounded. He had been on Peleliu for just under two hours.

CHAPTER 7

Death in the Afternoon

The *Time/Life* correspondent Tom Lea had arrived on Orange Beach 3 with the third wave, but the enemy fire had lost little of its intensity:

'Mortar shells *whished* and *whapped* through the air over our heads; they hit without apparent pattern on the beach and in the reef at our backs. Turning my head seaward, I saw a direct hit on an LVT; pieces of iron and men seemed to sail slow-motion into the air, as bursts began to creep steadily from the reef in towards the beach. The shells from one mortar rustled through the air directly over our heads at intervals of a few seconds, bursting closer and closer. Then a flat cracking flash nearly buried me with sand; wiggling out and trying to wipe the sharp grains from my sweating eyelids, I saw in the clinging gray smoke that a burst had hit about six feet from my left foot.

'A different kind of shell-burst began to come at us from a new direction, we judged that it was 75mm artillery from a Jap battery down the beach on a peninsula to our right. We saw hits on five or six LVTs as they came jolting in over the reef; as I looked over my shoulder a burst smashed into a file of Marines wading towards our beach from a smoking LVT – Jap machine guns lashed the reef with white lines and Marines fell with a bloody splash into green water.'

The '0–1 line' for the 7th Regiment – the boundary that was expected to be reached by the end of day one – reached across to the east coast of Peleliu and included the south-west promontory (Ngarmoked Island) and the unnamed island south of Orange 3. The ferocity of the enemy opposition, and the fact that some of the 3rd Battalion had been forced to land alongside the 5th Regiment on Orange 2, caused some modification to this plan; however, by 9.30am two companies of the 3/7th were heading eastward. Within an hour they had arrived at a large concrete blockhouse and the advance ground to a halt; tanks had been assigned to the unit to assist with the reduction of this obstacle, but in their swing to the left the Shermans had become attached to the 5th Regiment by mistake, and it was some time before they located the 3/7th.

The 1st Battalion, under Lt.Col. John Gormley, had landed north of their assigned sector, but soon regrouped and headed east into an area of mangrove swamp. The single trail through the swamp was heavily defended by numerous pillboxes and 'spider traps' – camouflaged holes for snipers – and the advance slowed to a snail's pace.

As the afternoon wore on the 7th Regiment were well short of their over-optimistic 0–1 line; the 3/7th were still held up at the blockhouse, and there was a wide gap on the left flank between them and the 5th Regiment. The southern end of the island, including Ngarmoked Island, was still occupied by the Japanese, who were directing heavy fire into the right flank of the Marines.

General Rupertus on the *DuPage* was becoming concerned about this loss of momentum, and decided to commit the divisional Reconnaissance Company as reinforcements. General Oliver Smith was later to comment in the official history: 'This company was thrown in on the right with the 1st Battalion [7th Marines] and suffered heavy casualties. This was an improper use of the Reconnaissance Company, as there later developed several opportunities for employment of this Company in the manner for which it had been trained.'

More worrying still was the decision to land the sole divisional reserve, the 2nd Battalion of the 7th Marines, even though there had been no request for them from either Oliver Smith or the regimental commander Col. Hanneken.

The battalion commander, Lt.Col. Spencer Berger, was ordered to take his men in landing craft to the Amtrac transfer line on the reef off Orange Beach 3 between 3.00pm and 4.00pm. Upon arrival he was told that the control officer had received no orders regarding landing this battalion, and was unable to contact Divisional HQ. Shortly before dark he attempted to get the men from the reef to the beach, but attracted such heavy enemy fire that the effort was aborted.

Berger was then ordered to return the battalion to their transport ship, the *Leedstown*. Predictably, this proved to be easier said than done: it was growing dark, few of the landing craft had compasses, and all the transports had moved further offshore for the night. In the early hours of the morning Lt.Col. Berger finally located the *Leedstown,* but the fiasco was not yet played out – the captain of the ship at first refused to allow the Marines back on board, as he had only received orders to land them. The rounding-up of the landing craft and re-embarkation took most of the night, but there was little respite for the weary Marines of the 2/7th. At 8.00am on 16 September they were off-loaded once more, to finally land on Peleliu some 15 hours after leaving the ship.

'I've shot my bolt when they go in', commented Rupertus to his chief of staff Col. Selden.

* * *

All of the Marines ashore were now beginning to suffer from an enemy nearly as lethal as the Japanese – heat and thirst. The heat on the island was incredibly intense as the sun reached its zenith; temperatures of 105°F in the shade were recorded (though there was little shade).

Most Marines had landed with two water canteens, but under these conditions they were soon used up. Lips cracked, faces blistered, the steel of weapons became too hot to touch, casualties from heat exhaustion far exceeded those from enemy action, and for the wounded awaiting evacuation the sweltering heat only compounded their misery. It was not until D+1 that water began to arrive from the offshore transports; this was stored in 55-gallon drums, and when the parched Marines began to drink it they discovered that the water was tainted with diesel fuel, causing many to become violently sick. An identical situation had occurred during the Tarawa landings in November 1943, when water from drums became undrinkable as a result of contamination; it seemed that little had been learned in the intervening year.

* * *

As the afternoon wore on a marked increase in the volume of Japanese artillery and mortar fire alerted the Marines inland from Orange Beaches 1 & 2 that something was brewing. A spotter plane covering the area north of the airfield reported Japanese tanks gathering in the foothills of the Umurbrogol beyond the barracks area.

Marine intelligence knew that the enemy had tanks on Peleliu – a tank company was a standard component of Japanese infantry divisions. The open ground around the airfield was the obvious place to deploy them, so appropriate measures had been taken. Some of the 37mm anti-tank guns from the regimental weapons company and light 75mm 'pack' howitzers from the 11th Marine Artillery had been landed near the 5th Regiment's positions, and three Shermans from Company B of the 1st Tank Battalion lay waiting.

Although the term was technically inaccurate, most Marines contemptuously referred to the Japanese Type 95 *Ha-Go* light tank as a 'tankette'; it weighed under 10 tons (in contrast to the 35-ton Sherman), and mounted one 37mm gun and two 7.7mm machine guns. Powered by a Mitsubishi 110hp diesel engine that gave a top speed of 28mph, the Type 95's most serious defect was thin armour – 14mm maximum, compared with 76mm on the Sherman. This meant that they were not only vulnerable to the rather elderly 37mm M3 anti-tank gun, and devastatingly so to Marine howitzers and the 75mm gun of the Sherman; with luck they could even be disabled by 0.50cal machine gun fire.

At around 4.50pm the Japanese began their counter-attack. Between 13 and 19 tanks accompanied by 400–500 infantry moved forward from the north of the airfield; but they had waited too long, and the Marines were prepared.

At first the advance was well co-ordinated and disciplined, with the tanks in two columns and the infantry well dispersed and taking advantage of what cover was available. Some clung to the turrets of tanks, others crouched behind; but as they reached about halfway across the airfield the tanks shot forward in what one Marine officer described as a 'Wild West cavalry charge', leaving the accompanying infantry behind in a cloud of dust. As they came within range the Marines opened up with 37mm anti-tank guns, bazookas, mortars, anti-tank rifle grenades and machine guns – even a Navy dive-bomber joined in, dropping a 500lb bomb into the centre of the mêlée. Tanks began to explode and burn all across the airfield, and the Japanese infantry were decimated by a hail of American gunfire. Now, from the south of the airfield, the Sherman platoon burst out into the open and joined the action.

Corpsman Jack McCombs watched as a Marine with a bazooka knocked out a Japanese tank: 'One Jap trying to get out of the tank was practically cut in half by machine guns, and as a joke the guys carried his pants with the parts of the legs in them and threw them to one another. I know it sounds gruesome, but it helped break the tension.' By September 1944 nearly all Allied soldiers had been affected by the dehumanising conditions of the Pacific War.

Still the survivors kept coming, and overran a narrow sector left of Company B before being wiped out. Marines in the front lines held their position even though some were wounded by fragments of exploding tanks in their midst, or were crushed to death under the onrushing machines. Lieutenant 'Pop' Hale of the 3rd Armored Amphibian Tractor Battalion gives a first-hand account of his part in the battle:

'With about 18 tanks they came rushing across the airfield in a cloud of dust, [and] we started hitting them with 37mm cannon fire and machine guns. We were firing at them with everything we had, but one came on; we finally knocked his track off with our 75s, causing him to swerve into a shell crater. A Marine infantryman nearby leapt from his foxhole and jumped on the turret of the tank, jerked open the hatch, and threw a grenade inside. Having trouble holding the hatch down, he calmly sat on it until the grenade exploded with such an impact that it boosted the Marine a good yard or so into space.

'As he hit the ground holding his behind, he had a very satisfied grin on his face.'

Exactly who destroyed what was to become a matter of heated debate after the engagement; so many tanks were hit from different directions by so many weapons that claims reached astronomical proportions – someone has estimated that if all the claims had been accepted at face value, 179½ Japanese tanks would have been destroyed. Whatever the claims, the attack was totally frustrated at a fearful cost to the enemy; when things quietened down 450 Japanese bodies were recovered from the airfield – the Marines had suffered 59 dead and wounded.

'One instance in this battle will always stand out in my mind', says R.Bruce Watkins. 'Near the end, there was a general milling about at the

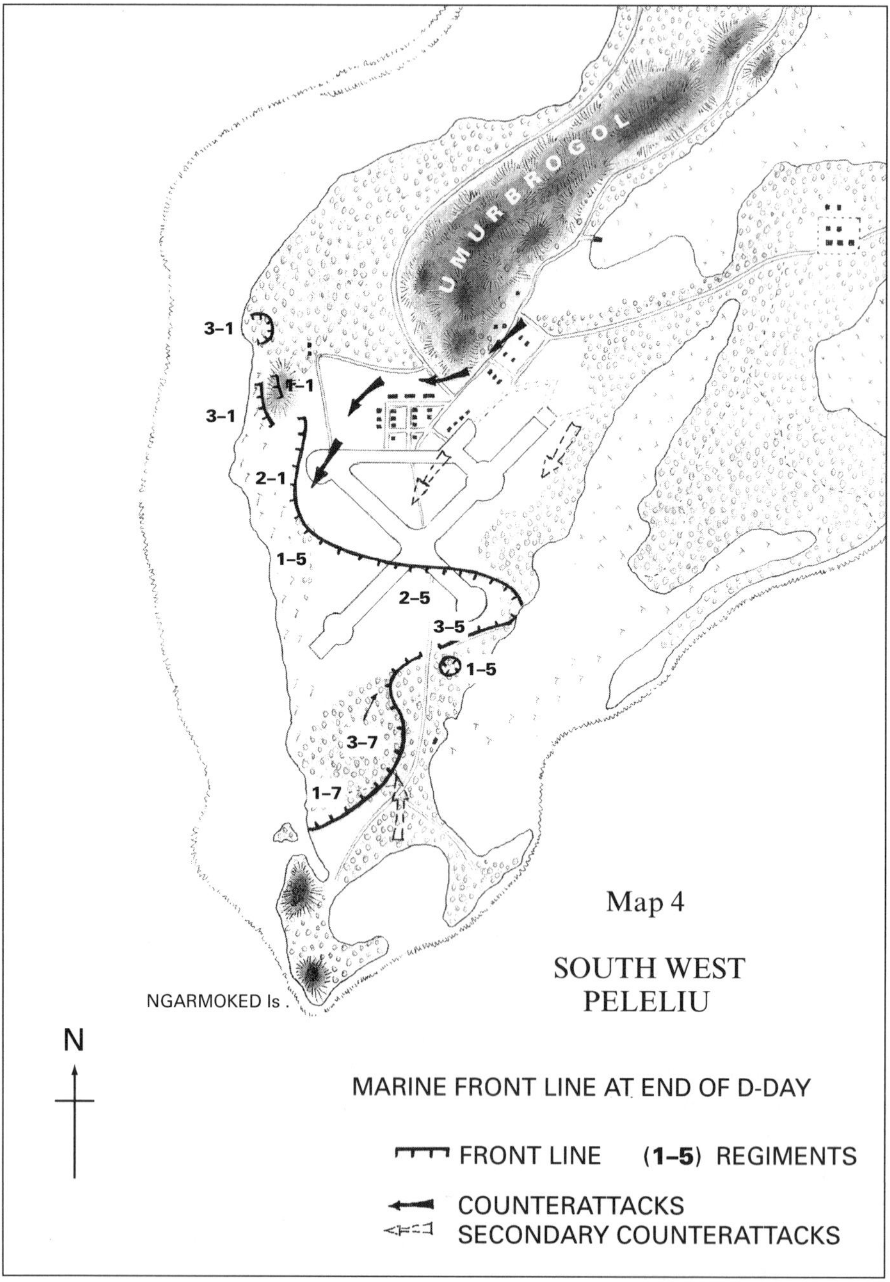

Map 4

SOUTH WEST PELELIU

far end of the airfield with our Shermans trying to zero in on the last three Jap tanks. One of the Japs got behind one of ours and was blazing away at the back of the Sherman; I remember screaming at our tank to look back (of course, there was no way for him to hear), when suddenly the Sherman's turret swivelled 180 degrees and let loose a 75mm round that blew the turret right off the Jap tank. It continued to run for a ways like a beheaded chicken.'

At the beginning of this action the Sherman crews, conventionally, fired solid armour-piercing shot, but this was seen to pass clean through the thinly-armoured Type 95s without apparent result. The Marine tankers then switched to high explosive rounds, which blew the Japanese machines apart so comprehensively that the number destroyed could not afterwards be counted with any certainty.

* * *

The enemy continued to mount attacks throughout the late afternoon. At 5.30pm an infantry group supported by what were probably the last two remaining tanks charged along the east–west taxiway of the airfield towards the junction of White 2 and Orange 1; both tanks were blown apart and the infantry were decimated. Other probing sorties were easily repulsed.

By the time the Marines were preparing to dig in for the night the 2nd Battalion of the 5th Regiment had fought their way across the southern boundary of the airfield and had almost reached the eastern swamp. Taking advantage of the enemy's disorganisation after the tank battle, they turned north and reached the centre of the airfield before encountering stiff opposition; here they decided to halt for the night. Jim Johnston took a dim view of the situation:

'Crossing the airfield lengthwise didn't really seem like the brightest thing I'd ever done . . . It meant charging across 200 yards of flat ground, completely exposed to an enemy who had all kinds of firepower and control of the high ground where he could watch every move we made.'

* * *

Meanwhile, on White Beaches 1 & 2, the 1st Regiment were still catching hell. The loss of their communications equipment meant that Puller could not call for reinforcements, and his need for them was much more urgent than Col. Hanneken's. In eight hours of some of the fiercest fighting of the battle the 1st Marines had made little headway against enemy troops entrenched on the ridge directly to their front where Lt.Col. Sabol's 3rd Battalion were pinned down.

Companies A and B of the 1st Battalion were committed in an attempt to clear the area between the ridge and the Point, where Capt. Hunt and the survivors of Company K of the 3/1st were still isolated; but neither force was able to close the gap. There were fears that a determined attack by the Japanese at this point might allow them to break through to the sea, with disastrous results. All available troops – 100 men from the 1st Engineer Battalion and some HQ personnel – were pressed forward to establish a secondary line to bolster this crucial point.

Five Amtanks from the 3rd Armored Amphibian Tractor Battalion had suffered severe damage landing on the White beaches that morning. Tank number 'B1' was hit by a 20mm shell which killed one machine gunner and wounded another; the Amtank then grounded and had to be abandoned. Number 'B2' was hit about 50 yards offshore and then again at the water's edge, where it caught fire. Lieutenant Robertson, the tank commander, was blown bodily out of the machine-gun well, one crew member was killed and another wounded; the vehicle was a total loss. 'B3' became part of the desperate effort to protect Capt. Hunt's beleaguered Company K at the Point. 'B4' was hit about 20 yards from the beach, wounding the port machine gunner; the tank later grounded on a tree stump and was abandoned. 'B5' was hit by a 77mm shell in the port pontoon; and two men in the cargo compartment were killed by mortar fire while awaiting evacuation from the beach. The Amtank only got 50 yards before sustaining several hits around the turret; the crew kept firing until smoke forced them to leave.

One of the wounded Marines evacuated to a hospital ship from White Beach 1 that afternoon was nineteen-year-old Pfc. Ivan Elms, the radioman from an Amtank in the vanguard of the 3rd Armored Amphibian Tractor Battalion. Elms had been manning a 0.30cal bow machine gun as he ploughed towards the shore that morning. The beach ahead looked far too empty, but he knew that the enemy were waiting somewhere behind their machine guns and their mortars. As they crossed the reef the water around them erupted; Elms's Amtank touched the sand and slowly ground across the beach, but at that instant a shell ripped through the vehicle. 'Let's get out of here!', he yelled to those who were still alive, and they piled out and sprinted across the beach.

Elms passed one man whose stomach was completely blown away, with only thin pieces of skin on either side holding him together. He made a wild charge for cover accompanied by other Marines; the sand in front of him *pop, pop, popped* as a machine gunner somewhere homed in on them. On his left a Marine lay in a pool of blood, riddled from his ankle to his throat by a burst. 'Mate, I need help', he cried; 'Do you know how to pray?' 'Pray? – I don't know how to pray', said Elms; and the man died looking him straight in the face.

Elms stumbled on to another man; this one had had his upper lip shot off but was still trying to smoke a cigarette. While Elms and a Corpsman tried to help him a jeep coming up behind them was hit; the vehicle and its two occupants literally disappeared – there was nothing left but smoke. Some of the debris from the explosion hit Elms and the Corpsman; Elms had a hole in his left knee about the size of a lemon, an artery was hanging out like a little finger and was pumping blood out onto the ground in rhythm with his heartbeat. 'I'm hit!', he cried to the Corpsman, but then he saw that the Corpsman's left arm was blown off. 'I'm sorry but I don't think I'll be able to help you', he said, and keeled over dead. It was some hours before Elms was evacuated from White 1.

* * *

Up on the Point, Capt. George Hunt's survivors were hanging on like grim death under a prolonged mortar barrage which sent shrapnel ricocheting around the rocks. Company K of the 3/1st was down to about 34 able-bodied men; the wounded were carried down to the water's edge in the hope that they could be evacuated by Amtrac. Water and ammunition were already in short supply; but their ordeal was to last another 30 hours before they could be retrieved.

Divisional deputy commander Gen. Oliver Smith, the senior officer ashore, had finally made contact with 'Chesty' Puller at around 1.00pm, when Puller's liaison officer dropped over the edge of Smith's command post in the tank trap and told him that the 1st Regiment CP was at the foot of a ridge some 300 yards to the north-east. Smith immediately sent a communications team to lay ground lines, and a phone link was working within 30 minutes.

Smith asked Puller about his situation and if he needed help. 'I'm alright', replied the colonel; 'maybe about 40 killed and wounded.' How he came by these figures is unclear; it may have been the result of misinformation, but the real figure was nearer 500.

General Smith had an unexpected visitor to his CP a little later when Maj.Gen. Roy Geiger, commander of III Amphibious Corps, slid down the side of the tank trap. Oliver Smith was astonished: 'Look here, General, according to the book you aren't supposed to be here at this time', he said.

Geiger replied that he wanted to know why those Amtracs were burning, and also wanted to see the airfield. After a brief discussion about casualties, Geiger asked, 'Where's Rupertus ?' 'He's still out there on the *DuPage* with his broken ankle', said Smith. Geiger, who had known nothing of this injury, was surprised and concerned: 'If I'd known that, I'd have relieved him'.

* * *

Lieutenant Carlton Rouh had come ashore on Orange 1 with his mortar platoon, and by 3.00pm they had worked their way to the edge of the airfield. They took shelter in a ditch parallel to one of the taxiways, and attempted to spot enemy guns at the base of the Umurbrogol on the far side of the airfield. At the end of the ditch was a dug-out, still smouldering after being burned out by a Marine flamethrower. Rouh's suspicions were aroused and he decided to investigate.

As he entered the dugout a shot rang out; at first he thought that his own gun had gone off accidentally, but a sharp pain in his abdomen soon changed his opinion. As other Marines from his platoon dashed forward, an enemy soldier crept out and pitched a hand grenade into their midst. Rouh lurched forward, pushing his men to one side, and flung himself on to the grenade, taking the full blast of the explosion himself.

One of his men straddled him and fired into the dug-out, killing 15 Japanese soldiers who tried to escape. Fortunately for the lieutenant, a Corpsman was nearby; he was rushed to an aid station where a surgeon was able to stop him from bleeding to death. Carlton Rouh recovered after prolonged hospital treatment, to be awarded the Medal of Honor and a promotion to captain.

* * *

Evening was now approaching, and the troops were looking for places to dig in for the night. Night fighting was not popular with the US Marines, but the Japanese revelled in it. Tom Lea with the 7th Regiment has vivid memories of that first night: 'About sundown we settled into our places at the end of a trench; the low sun cast a sulphurous yellow light through the smoke, then faded. We settled down to sleep as close to Mother Earth as we could get. Mosquitoes began to swarm and bite; we expected that it might cool off after sundown, but we were wrong.

'Little balls of fire danced under my eyelids when I closed my eyes, flurries of gunfire rattled and thumped. I don't know what time it was when the counter-attack came; there was a sudden flurry of rifle fire and blatting machine guns, a sudden pause, and then a crashing answer of fire from somewhere out in the blackness ahead of our trench. Small arms fire ahead of us became a continuous rattle. Abruptly three star shells burst in the sky, then the howitzers just behind us opened up, shaking the ground with their blasts. Jap mortars spotted them and bursts came our way, some came very close but I don't know what casualties they caused. Then I heard, in pauses between bursts of fire, the high-pitched screaming yells of the Japs as they charged – I don't know how long it took the Marines to beat the Japs back, perhaps it was an hour, perhaps longer.

'Next day we learned more about what the Japs had done during the night. The nearest dead ones had been found at 30 yards in front of our position; Japs wearing helmets of dead Marines had sneaked into foxholes behind our front line and cut throats, they had been slashed or shot by Marines in hand-to-hand fighting in the darkness and there were bodies now in the morning light.' (The Marine helmets, with their spotted cloth camouflage covers, were particularly distinctive; in the darkness the rest of the uniform – khaki for the Japanese, and drab green dungarees for the Marines – was harder to make out.)

* * *

Gen. Oliver Smith stayed in command on the first night. His men held a beachhead some 3,000 yards in length and averaging 500 yards in depth; in the centre, a penetration of 1,500 yards had been made to the mangrove inlet which effectively marked the far side of the island (*see* Map 4). The 0–1 line, always an optimistic target, had not been achieved, but there was a good foothold in the southern sector. The 11th Marine Artillery had one and a half battalions of 75mm pack howitzers and more than a battalion of 105mm howizers ashore and in position. American casualties were reckoned at 210 men killed and 901 wounded; in addition, there were a very high number of cases of heat prostration and some of battle fatigue.

Most of the American casualties had been suffered by 'Chesty' Puller's 1st Regiment. As one tankman put it, 'When the tide went out that night, you could have walked 300 yards across that beach on bodies of dead Marines'.

The Japanese version of the day's battle was startlingly different: according to Col.Tokechi Tada's Central Pacific Area Operational Records, 'By 1000 hours our forces successfully put the enemy to rout' . . . 'At 2.20pm the enemy again attempted to make the perilous landing on the south-western part of our coastline; the units in that area repulsed the daring counter-attack and put the enemy to rout once more. However, in another sector of the coastline near Ayame [Orange 3] the enemy, with the aid of several tanks, were successful in landing, although they were encountering heavy losses inflicted by our troops.'

If this was Col. Nakagawa's understanding of the situation from his command post in the ridges overlooking the airfield, then he appeared to have a confused picture of the day's events.

Night brought little relief for the exhausted Marines, straining their ears in the darkness of their hasty foxholes; the Japanese continued to shell and mortar the American lines. At the Point an Amtrac had at last succeeded in bringing ammunition, water, grenades and food to George Hunt's beleaguered men, but they had to fight a running battle against Japanese infiltrators throughout the night; daylight would reveal the bodies of dozens of enemy soldiers who had attempted to prise them from their coral citadel.

CHAPTER 8

The Second Round

'Our glorious forces have again slaughtered thousands of bloodthirsty American Marines in a stupid invasion attempt, this time in the Palau Islands. Commanded by valiant and brilliant Colonel Kunio Nakagawa, superb and valorous Japanese troops bravely frustrated the daring landings by 1000hrs, putting the screaming enemy hordes to flight.

'At 1400hrs, the ill-fated butchers attempted again to make a landing on the south-west tip of our coastline. This frantic and disorganised counter-attack was also repulsed and the fiendish Yankees were put to rout once more, with the sea red with their blood.'

Radio Tokyo's colourful version of the Peleliu invasion may have brought joy to the hearts of the Japanese public, but it had little basis in reality.

The Marine objectives for 16 September – D+1 – were unambiguous. In the north the 1st Regiment were expected to secure the ridgeline to their front, bridge the gap on the left and make contact with Capt. Hunt and his men on the Point; while on the right they would seize the northern portion of the airfield and, in conjunction with the left flank of the 5th Regiment, swing northward to the foothills of the Umurbrogol.

In the centre, the 5th Marines would devote almost all of their efforts to occupying the airfield and the associated buildings; but they would also consolidate their foothold on the far side of the island, thus isolating the enemy on their right flank.

In the south, the 7th Marines were to finish off the enemy in the southern peninsula, a task that the planners had hoped would be completed on the first day.

General Rupertus and his staff came ashore at around 9.50am on 16 September, with his foot still in plaster and using a walking stick. Arriving at Oliver Smith's CP in the anti-tank ditch, he was briefed on the current situation. He was particularly irritated by the news from the 1st Marines, calling Col. Puller on the field telephone to demand, 'Can't you move any faster? – Goddammit, Lewie, you've got to kick asses to get results'. Clearly he had little grasp of the true situation on White Beaches 1 & 2, and was frustrated that his pre-invasion predictions were falling apart.

The 'tank trap CP' would remain the nerve centre of the battle until the whole of southern Peleliu was in American hands; it would then move to what had originally been the Japanese administration building near the airfield. General Oliver Smith would continue to use the tank trap CP until early November, when he returned to Pavuvu. The attitude of Rupertus to his second-in-command had changed little: Gen. Smith was to spend most of his time chasing around the various command posts gathering information for the immobile general, but was never asked to sit in on any of the planning meetings at his headquarters – an extraordinary omission, given that one Japanese shell could have put him in command of the division at a moment's notice.

* * *

The temperature, which had hovered in the region of 100°F on D-Day, promised to go even higher on the 16th; by mid-morning it was 105, and by the afternoon it would peak at 115°F. D+1 was to see cases of heat exhaustion, sunstroke, and stomach problems from drinking contaminated water escalate to near-epidemic proportions (it would not be until D+5 that the 1st Engineer Battalion would discover that fresh water could be drilled almost anywhere on the island).

No record exists of how many Marines were disabled by the heat, but it certainly ran into the hundreds, while dozens were evacuated with vomiting, stomach cramps and diarrhoea from the water contamination.

With the heat came the smells. Dead Marines were quickly removed to the beach area, but the Japanese bodies were left where they fell, and the heat soon turned them into stinking, swollen, fly-blown horors that the Marines avoided like the plague – where they had any choice. Captain George Hunt described the bodies around his positions on the Point: 'A sickening, putrid stench was emanating from the ones we had killed yesterday, their yellow skins were beginning to turn brown, and their fly-ridden corpses, still free of maggots, were already cracked and bloated like rotten melons'.

During the previous night the Japanese had mounted an almost continuous series of attacks on the Point, but these had been repulsed at great cost to themselves and to the Marines.

With daylight arrived Amtracs delivering ammunition, supplies and some reinforcements to Hunt's still-isolated Company K; they landed at the rocky extremity of the Point under enemy fire, and on the return trip evacuated his wounded to the relative safety of White Beach 1.

Bloody fighting in this area continued throughout the morning and afternoon of D+1, as the regimental reserve, the 1/1st Marines under Maj. Raymond Davis, battled to close the gap between Hunt and the main body of the 1st Regiment. Major Davis had been wounded in the leg within minutes of landing, but continued in command of his battalion. The opposition was fierce; the Japanese, entrenched in their camouflaged pillboxes, stubbonly refused to yield an inch while they had one man left alive with one round for his weapon. With the assistance of two Sherman tanks the Marines finally succeeded in securing a 500-yard stretch of the ridge; this gave them leverage, and they would finally bridge the gap cutting off Company K on the morning of D+2.

Hunt and his gallant Marines had by then been isolated for over 30 hours, and at one time had been reduced to 18 able-bodied men; from the 235 men in the company, only 78 of the original complement remained. Hunt was later awarded the Navy Cross, much to the dismay of his men – who felt that if ever there was a certain candidate for the Medal of Honor it was George P.Hunt.

On the 1st Regiment's right, meanwhile, Lt.Col. Honsowetz's 2nd Battalion had jumped off at 8.30am and made excellent progress across the north of the airfield, reaching the eastern taxiway circle in just over half an hour. Linking up with the left flank of the 5th Marines, at around noon they reached the built-up area at the foot of the Umurbrogol ridges. Here they were engaged in fierce hand-to-hand fighting among the ruins of the barracks and airfield buildings which had earlier been pounded into chaos by the naval bombardment and air strikes. Lieutenant R.Bruce Watkins of the 2/1st's Company E witnessed the action in this area:

'Across the airfield we approached a barracks area, where we were stopped by heavy fire from a large round concrete bunker approximately 50 feet in diameter. We tried anti-tank grenades to no avail; I remember watching Sgt. John Kincaid as if in slow motion creep up to a firing slot, pull the pin on a grenade, and flip it in. It was thrown or bounced back at once, just as deliberately, and in spite of the five-second fuze, John picked it up again and thrust it into the aperture – this time it went off, but despite his valiant effort firing quickly resumed.

'Lieutenant Lee Height of the 2nd Platoon thought that perhaps a tank could do the job and ran back to get their attention, returning with a Sherman in tow. He pointed to the firing ports; the tank had fired perhaps two rounds when the most unbelievable action occurred. All of us were hugging the ground . . . watching the tank when we heard the whine of a Navy dive-bomber coming directly at us. To this day I believe that the pilot mistook us for Japs, but he released his bomb, probably a 500-pounder, and we all watched as it headed towards us in a slight arc. Sure that we were going to be decimated, we could only hug the ground and pray; miraculously the bomb hit dead centre on the bunker, collapsing it and killing all the Japanese within. The blast stunned us and covered us with white coral dust; we got shakily to our feet like so many ghosts, in great wonder to be alive – no one had been hit.'

* * *

When a Japanese shell howled through the air and exploded in the 5th Regiment CP near the edge of the airfield, the CO, Col. 'Bucky' Harris, was almost buried but escaped with a badly wrenched knee and a strained back. Although he was not seriously wounded the regimental

Maj.Gen. Julian C.Smith was designated Commander US Expeditionary Troops for Operation Stalemate 2. The previous November he had commanded the 2nd Marine Division in the assault on Tarawa. (US National Archives)

Maj.Gen. Roy S.Geiger, Commander III Amphibious Corps for the Peleliu operation. On D-Day he appeared without warning in Oliver Smith's command post in a Japanese anti-tank ditch - 'Look here, General, according to the book you aren't supposed to be here . . .'. (USMC)

Maj.Gen. William H.Rupertus, commanding the 1st Marine Division on Peleliu. Before the battle he assured his regimental commanders, 'This is going to be a fast one – we'll be through in three days.' At its height he tearfully told one of them, 'I'm at the end of my rope . . . You usually seem to know what to do – I'm going to turn over to you everything we have left.' (USMC)

(Above) *Brig.Gen. Oliver P.Smith, the deputy commander of the 1st Marine Division, who bore much of the burden of planning the operation and was the senior officer ashore on the morning of D-Day. Inexplicably, Gen. Rupertus froze him out of command discussions: 'I was never consulted about anything tactical.' (Marine Corps Historical Center)*

(Above right) *Col. Lewis 'Chesty' Puller, the much-decorated regimental commander of the 1st Marines. To a signal asking about his progress at Bloody Nose Ridge he would reply, 'We're still going, but some of my companies are damn small.' By D+2 his regiment had taken 50 per cent casualties. (USMC)*

(Right) *Pte. Charles Owen, photographed at 'Boot Camp' when he was just 14 years old. He was 16 when he landed on Orange Beach 3 with Company A of the 7th Marines, and enountered Maj. Charles M.Parker of the amphibious tank battalion: 'This crazy sonofabitch is going to kill me if I don't get the hell off this beach!' (Charles H.Owen)*

(Above) *Operation Desecrate 1, 30–31 March 1944. Japanese shipping can be seen burning and sinking; at extreme left is a US Navy F6F Hellcat. This operation by Adm. Marc 'Oklahoma Pete' Mitscher's Task Force 58 destroyed Japanese naval and air power in the Palau Islands. (US National Archives)*

(Below) *D-Day, 15 September 1944: aerial view looking east and south, with fires from the bombardment burning on the airfield and in the woodlands inland from the White and Orange invasion beaches. Compare this view with Map 3 on page 52: at top centre can be seen Ngarmoked Island, left of it the south-east promontory, and right of it the 'unnamed island'. Note the pale effect of the shallow water over the reef in the foreground. (US Navy)*

(Above) *D-Day: landing craft fitted with banks of 4.5in rockets deliver the last element of the bombardment from close inshore. (US Navy)*

(Below) *D-Day: ahead of the assault companies in the first landing craft, Marine 'Amtanks' of the 3rd Armored Amphibian Tractor Battalion head towards the concealing bank of smoke and dust which hung over the beaches. When it cleared, many of them would be seen wrecked and burning. The nearest vehicle is an LVT(A)-1, mounting the turret and 37mm gun from a Stuart tank; the others, apparently from Company A, are LVT(A)-4s with the open-topped turret and short 75mm gun from the M8 Howitzer Motor Carriage. (US Navy)*

(Above) *LVT-2 'Amtracs' carry assault infantry towards the shore. To judge by their uncovered helmets with hand-painted camouflage, these are not Marines but Army GIs, so the photo may have been taken during the Angaur landings by the 81st Division on 17 September. (US Navy)*

(Below) *D-Day: aerial view of the 1st and 3rd Battalions of the 1st Marines landing on White Beaches 1 and 2 – 'the Point' is at the top of the picture, enfilading White Beach 1 at short range. (US Navy)*

(Above) *D-Day: oily black smoke rises from burning Amtanks, Amtracs and DUKWs. The line of white water marks the edge of the reef, where succeeding waves of infantry were forced to wait to be transferred from Higgins boats to Amtracs for the journey in through the shallows. The viewpoint, again, is east and south from above the White and Orange beaches (US Navy)*

(Below) *D-Day: Marines take cover around LVT(A)-4 number B-6, disabled on top of a Japanese emplacement just inland from White Beach 2. (USMC)*

(Above) *One of the 5th Regiment's 37mm M3 anti-tank guns. Note the massive construction of the shell-pocked concrete bunker at left, hardly damaged by the naval bombardment. (USMC)*

(Below) *Wreckage of two of the Type 95* Ha-Go *tanks destroyed during the Japanese counter-attack across the airfield on the afternoon of D-Day. (USMC)*

(Above) *Marines examine the ruins of the Japanese barracks area north of the airfield, where the 2nd Battalion of the 1st Marines saw heavy fighting. (USMC)*

(Below) *Japanese dead litter the perimeter of the airfield after the savage fighting on D-Day, in the course of which the 5th Marines had to assault across open ground into a withering fire. (USMC)*

(Left) *Maj.Gen. Paul J.Mueller, US Army, commander of the 81st Division – the 'Wildcats'. Angaur was their first taste of combat; soon afterwards they were committed to the reduction of the Umurbrogol Pocket on Peleliu. (US Army)*

(Below) *Angaur seen from the air, looking south-west from Beach Red, where the 322nd Infantry landed on 17 September – compare with Map 5 on page 104. At top right can be seen the lighthouse on Palomas Hill, and left of it the large buildings of the phosphate plant. (US Navy)*

(Above) *Crews from an LVT(A)-1 and an LVT(A)-4 of the 3rd Armored Amphibian Tractor Bn examine one of the Japanese barges which brought reinforcements of Maj. Iida's 2/15th Infantry across from Babelthuap to northern Peleliu on the nights of D+7 and D+9. (USMC)*

(Below) *This aerial photo of southern Peleliu was taken some years after the war, when vegetation had grown back vigorously. Note the Umurbrogol area between the white lines of the West and East Roads, at centre left; the regrown foliage again masks the true nature of the terrain, just as it did in reconnaissance photos in 1944. (US Air Force)*

(Above) *F4U Corsair of Maj. 'Cowboy' Stout's VMF-114 dropping napalm over the crags of the Umurbrogol Pocket; note the appalling terrain and often sheer cliffs. These missions must have been the shortest of the war: the fighter-bombers shuttled between the target and Peleliu airfield only a few hundred yards away – some pilots did not bother to retract the undercarriage. (USMC)*

(Right) *The* Time/Life *correspondent and war artist Tom Lea, who came ashore on D-Day with the 7th Marines on Orange Beach 3: 'I saw a wounded man near me, staggering in the direction of the LVTs, his face was half bloody pulp and the mangled shreds of what was left of an arm hung down like a stick as he bent over in his stumbling, shock-crazed walk. The half of his face that was still human had the most terrible look of abject patience I have ever seen.'* See *his sketch on page 64. (USMC)*

(Above) *'Going in – first wave – I saw a Marine, his face painted for the jungle, his eyes set for the beach, his mouth set for murder.' (Tom Lea/ US Army Center for Military History)*

(Below) *'The blockhouse – looking up at the head of the trail I could see the big blockhouse that commanded the height.' (Tom Lea/ US Army Center for Military History)*

(Left) *'Side bay in a shellhole – the Padre read "I am the resurrection and the life".' (Tom Lea/US Army Center for Military History)*

(Below) *'Artillery support – at the southern end our artillerymen had dug holes and carried 75mm howitzers to the sites.' The foreground man in this 11th Marines gun crew wears the large naval 'talker's' helmet which accommodated a radio headset. (Tom Lea/ US Army Center for Military History)*

(Above) *The 94 survivors of Company A, 1st Battalion, 7th Marines before leaving Peleliu for Pavuvu. The company had landed on D-Day with 235 men. (Charles H.Owen)*

(Below) *Sherman tanks and infantry penetrate the blackened heart of the Umurbrogol Pocket – 'the Horseshoe' – compare with Map 8, page 143. We are looking north; the 'Fresh Water Pond' is in the right foreground, the 'Five Brothers' on the left, 'Hill 140' in the centre background, and 'Walt Ridge' on the right. In the later stage of the battle many Japanese were killed attempting to get water from the pond by night. (USMC)*

The American Military Cemetery on Peleliu during its dedication in 1944. A photo taken from the same angle in 1992 shows the obelisk intact but the whole area reclaimed by vegetation. (US National Archives)

Tom Climie of the 321st RCT and his wife Shirley dedicate the Wildcats' memorial on Angaur on 29 December 1995. Reportedly it has been well cared-for in the years since. (Tom Climie)

(Above) *The rusting hulk of one of the 710th Tank Battalion's Shermans now forms part of the breakwater on Angaur. (David M.Green)*

(Below) *Japanese defenders still occupying one of the hundreds of caves in the Umurbrogol, now shrouded in tropical vegetation once again. (Eric Mailander)*

commander's incapacity was to cause problems. His executive officer, Lt.Col. Lewis Walt, was obliged to act as his deputy, making the minor decisions and carrying out the 'legwork', while from his CP Harris would retain command of the regiment – an arrangement that was to continue until late in the battle. 'Harris could not get to the front lines. The less important decisions I made on my own, in the case of major decisions I talked the matter over with Colonel Harris. In the later stages of the campaign I ran the regiment from a forward CP, Colonel Harris stayed at the rear CP, and I kept him informed of what was going on,' said Walt.

The 5th Regiment's attack across the airfield had all the hallmarks of a First World War battle: rows of infantry advancing across flat open ground against an entrenched enemy in elevated, prepared positions. One Marine classed this attack as his worst experience of the entire war – shimmering heat, deafening noise, shells whistling and exploding all around, tracer bullets flashing past at waist height, steel splinters falling like rain, men stumbling and falling. Naval gunfire against Japanese emplacements north of the airfield appeared to have had minimal effect, and the volume of fire lashing down on the advancing Marines did not diminish.

The advance gained momentum as the halfway point was reached; there was no going back, and the best way to end the ordeal was to get forward and off the airfield as soon as possible. The plan was to push across the airfield and swing north to join up with the flank of the 1st Regiment.

The Marines saw wrecked Japanese aircraft, many destroyed during the pre-invasion raids, and in the distance the skeletons of the hangars, largely unrepaired since the devastating attacks by Task Force 58 at the end of March. Amtracs, shielded by tanks, brought up the rear and retrieved some of the wounded; many were not so lucky, and bled to death in the searing heat.

Men of the 1/5th Marines under the command of Lt.Col. Robert Boyd reached the hangar area, to find Japanese dug in among the aircraft revetments and anti-tank ditches; a series of fierce hand-to-hand actions began as the Marines prised them out of their strongpoints one by one. Casualties had been heavy; at 10.18am a message was sent back to Col. Harris asking for reinforcements, and at 11.40am the colonel sent another company of the 5th up to add weight to the attack. On their left flank, in the centre of the 1st Regiment, men of the 2nd and 3rd Battalions beat the enemy back far enough to gain control of part of the road that skirted the north of the airfield.

Corpsman Brooking Gex had set up his aid station at the northern end of one of the runways: 'About half a dozen stretcher bearers worked with me; as fast as they brought in men torn apart by shrapnel and bullets, I applied sulpha and battle packs. The Japanese snipers began picking off stretcher bearers, they were easy targets. Shells exploded all around us and screams echoed from victims as they lay in pools of blood, dismembered, entangled in their gear. Men fell faster than we could reach them. Hopelessness overwhelmed me and the line of stretchers seemed to stretch into infinity. "God help me", I gasped, "I don't think I can do anything for these men".

'And then, one after another, four men were gunned down trying to reach a Marine who looked like he would not make it. Finally I ran to the wounded man myself. His condition was desperate, the hole in his middle was the size of my fists held side by side – his stomach was leaking from this hole.'

*   *   *

About a mile to the south, the 7th Regiment, supported by tanks, began the task of clearing the southern peninsula – the southern promontory leading to Ngarmoked Island, the 'Unnamed Island', and the south-east promontory.

The first obstacle was a fortification comprising three dual-purpose gun positions and a blockhouse in a barracks area; the guns were soon overwhelmed, but the Japanese in the blockhouse still held out. Behind walls of 5-foot-thick reinforced concrete the enemy appeared to be invulnerable: naval gunfire was called in but could make no impression, 75mm shells from the Sherman tanks just bounced off the sides, covered gunports foiled the flamethrowers, and infantry weapons were useless. Finally a team of demolition experts were brought forward and, working under the cover of smoke, they succeeded in blasting the strongpoint into submission. By 9.25am part of Company I of the 3/7th had got across the island to the eastern shore, where they were soon fighting off determined enemy counter-attacks from the nearby mangrove swamps. Correspondent Tom Lea was with a patrol that came across the blockhouse shortly after it had been silenced:

'We could hear the heavy slugging of the tanks and mortars and howitzers, our cracking gunfire and the answering fire of the Japs just ahead as we came into an open pocket near the top of a gentle slope we were climbing. The clearing was a Jap barracks surrounded by small pillboxes and anti-tank positions; it was a smoking heap of rubble as we came to it, everything in it was smashed, twisted, blasted. There were dead Japs on the ground where they had been hit, and in two of the pillboxes I saw some of the bodies were nothing more than red meat and blood mixed with the gravelly dust of concrete and splintered logs.

'The Japs had cleared a trail from their barracks to the top of a ridge where their strongpoints were; we walked carefully up the side of this trail littered with Jap pushcarts, smashed ammunition boxes, rusty wire, old clothes and tattered gear – booby traps kept us from handling any of it. Looking up at the head of the trail I could see the big Jap blockhouse that commanded the height; the thing was now a great jagged lump of concrete, smoking. I saw our lead man meet a front line detail posted by the blockhouse while the other troops advanced down the hill with the three tanks and the flamethrowers. Isolated snipers were at work on our slope; small groups of Marines fanned out on both sides of the trail to clean them out while we climbed towards the blockhouse.'

At the southern tip of this sector the Japanese had constructed a honeycomb of pillboxes and trenches in the belief that the Americans would attempt an amphibious landing. The only advantage to the Marines was the fact that most of these installations faced seaward and could be assaulted from the flank or the rear. By 10.25am the forward patrols were within sight of the southern promontory; two pillboxes barred their way but were soon overwhelmed, and the promontory lay open to the Marines of the 1/7th.

The searing heat had taken its toll. The troops were dehydrated and exhausted from their protracted efforts; some men were literally speechless, their tongues so swollen that they could neither speak nor swallow. Under these circumstances it was decided to call it a day; the Marines found shelter as best they could amid the hard coral while supplies of water, food and ammunition were brought forward. Engineers cleared enemy mines and booby traps that barred the way across the sand spit leading to Ngarmoked Island; and as darkness approached, tanks arrived to support the next day's advance.

The 17-year-old Jeb Lord was with the 1st Battalion: 'Our company commander assigned five of us to carry a message to Battalion HQ, the strength of the group was due to the knowledge that we had bypassed some enemy and they were still in our rear. I was leading the group along a trail in fairly thick woods when a shot rang out and a green leaf floated down in front of my face. Before the leaf hit the ground I was flat on my face, looking up the ridge to my left where the shot came from. I saw several Japanese helmets looking over the ridge to where we lay; I aimed for the first one on the left and fired a round, [and] he raised up to almost full height and fell over backwards – I had shot my first enemy.'

The offshore Unnamed Island which had proved so troublesome to the 7th Regiment's right flank on D-Day was now dealt with. The main gun battery had been located by spotters from Orange Beach 3, and tanks moved in and knocked it out. A patrol went across at low tide and confirmed that the tanks had done a good job: not a single Japanese was found alive. However, during the night the enemy made several attempts to re-occupy the island. Naval star shells revealed a large number of troops wading across from Ngarmoked Island; Marine machine gunners had a field day, and there would be no more Japanese attacks from this area during the battle.

* * *

By nightfall on D+1, Gen. Rupertus was feeling more buoyant. The targets set out for the first day had almost been achieved, albeit a day late. A line from the Point on the west to the east coast just north of the airfield marked the northern extent of the Marine advance; in the south only Ngarmoked Island and a small portion of the south-east promontory were still in Japanese hands. The general believed that a rapid advance up the East and West Roads would pinch out the Umurbrogol, which could then be mopped up at will, leaving only the occupation of Ngesebus Island with its half-finished fighter strip to virtually complete the operation.

He was unaware that the battle for Peleliu had barely started.

CHAPTER 9

Wildcats on Angaur

The planners of Operation Stalemate gave two reasons for the occupation of Angaur. The first was to prevent the Japanese from using the island to reinforce the garrison on Peleliu during the Marine landings; and the second was that they wanted to build a bomber airfield on the low-lying ground in the south. As the situation developed, neither reason was to prove compelling.

The initial fear that the Japanese had a large garrison on Angaur turned out to be incorrect: the only troops on the island were about 1,400 men mainly of the 1st Battalion, 59th Infantry Regiment commanded by Maj. Ushio Goto. The choice of Angaur as a front-line bomber station was also short-sighted; although the Seabees and the Army's Corps of Engineers completed the task of building the airfield in an amazing five weeks, the rapid advance through the Philippines and events in other theatres meant that the Angaur base became superfluous.

Lying 6 miles south-west of Peleliu and measuring only 5,000 yards by 4,000 yards, the island was shaped roughly like a playing card 'spade'; it was predominantly flat apart from a 200-foot-high area in the north-west called Ramuldo Hill and an isolated hillock north of Saipan Town called Palomas Hill.

Major Goto's dilemma was how to defend the multitude of possible landing sites with his diminutive force. He decided that a flat area in the south-east (which the Americans had designated Green Beaches 2 & 3) was the most likely target, and proceeded to construct concrete and steel bunkers, pillboxes and machine gun emplacements, and to site anti-boat guns and minefields all along this 1,400-yard stretch. American intelligence coupled with aerial reconnaissance soon located these defences, and the invasion beaches were selected elsewhere.

The invasion of Angaur was to be an Army operation. The 81st Division, the 'Wildcats', under Maj.Gen. Paul Mueller, had been re-formed in 1942 at Camp Rucker in Alabama. They trained at Camp Horn, Arizona, and Camp San Luis Obispo and Camp Beale in California, before shipping out to Oahu in Hawaii. Amphibious training followed off Cape Esperance on Guadalcanal; and the division eventually sailed for the Palaus around the same time as the Marines.

The 81st remained afloat during the landings on Peleliu. On D-Day they manoeuvred close to the main northern island of Babelthuap, where they loaded troops into landing craft and formed up as if to invade, but then returned to their transports – all part of a feint to distract Gen. Inoue and his staff from the Peleliu invasion. On D+1, 16 September, the situation on Peleliu was considered to be sufficiently stable for the Angaur operation to go ahead. Admiral Fort, in command of the Navy invasion fleet, and III Amphibious Corps commander Gen. Geiger, issued the orders for the following morning.

Though there were minor differences of organisation and equipment, an Army infantry division was essentially similar to a Marine division: a 'triangular' force built around three regiments, each of three battalions, with additional artillery, engineer, armoured and other specialist units which could be divided up and attached to make the infantry regiments more or less self-sufficient. When this process was implemented the resulting three reinforced infantry regiments were termed Regimental Combat Teams (RCTs). Those of the 81st Division were the 321st, 322nd and 323rd RCTs, but only two were committed to the attack on Angaur; the 323rd were to remain in reserve.

At 8.00am on the morning of 17 September the battleship USS *Tennessee*, together with the heavy cruiser *Minneapolis* and the light cruisers *Denver*, *Cleveland* and *Columbus*, began the bombardment of the selected invasion beaches, firing hundreds of tons of 14in and 8in shells into the landing areas. Forty Dauntless dive-bombers from the carrier *Wasp* swept the beaches and the woodlands behind them; and as the infantry headed for the shore, converted LCIs blasted off 2,000 rounds of screaming 4.5in rockets. For the landings, Amtracs were provided by the Army's 726th Amphibian Tractor Battalion, and Amtanks by the 776th Amphibian Tank Battalion. Thomas Climie, a sergeant with the Service Company of the 321st Infantry, was there:

'The morning of September 17th, most of us said our prayers and waited. When we got the word we went over the side, down the nets, and into the landing craft. Some guys in our company had a small monkey and a chimp – the size of an eight- or ten-year old kid – they would climb and pass us on the ship's landing nets like we were standing still. I was in the third wave, and this was something to remember; each wave of landing craft kept going around in circles waiting for the word to go ashore. Men were crying, praying, some laughing.

'I got ashore, found a shellhole and dove into it; there was machine gun fire, rifle fire, mortars, light artillery, everyone yelling and screaming. We had landed on Blue Beach; I carefully worked my way inland taking advantage of any cover I could use, a rock here, a bush there – believe me, I aged ten years that day. As much as you prepare yourself you cannot come near to reality.'

There were two invasion beaches (see Map 5, page 104): Red in the north-east where the 322nd RCT were to land, and Blue about 2,000 yards further south, where Tom Climie and the 321st had come ashore. The plan was for the 322nd, under Col. Benjamin Venable, to move quickly

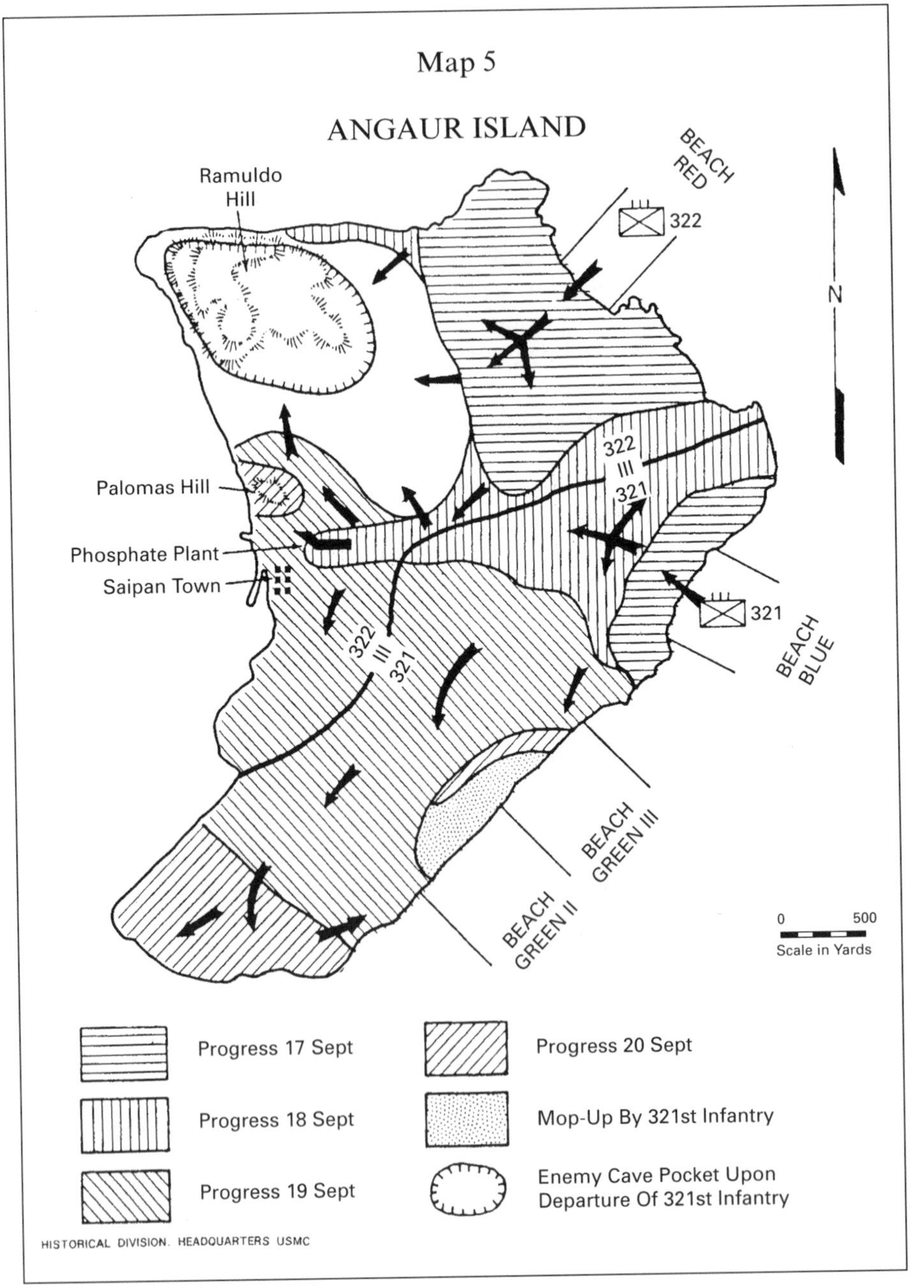
Map 5
ANGAUR ISLAND
Ramuldo Hill
BEACH RED
322
N
322
III
321
Palomas Hill
Phosphate Plant
Saipan Town
321
BEACH BLUE
322
III
321
BEACH GREEN III
BEACH GREEN II
0
500
Scale in Yards
Progress 17 Sept
Progress 18 Sept
Progress 19 Sept
Progress 20 Sept
Mop-Up By 321st Infantry
Enemy Cave Pocket Upon Departure Of 321st Infantry
HISTORICAL DIVISION. HEADQUARTERS USMC

south-west towards the main built-up area, Saipan Town, while the 321st, under Col. Robert Dark, pushed due west. They were to join up near the centre of the island before swinging south for the final drive.

The landings developed smoothly in the north. The first Amtracs came ashore on Red Beach at 8.35am against a few mortar rounds and some scattered small arms fire; the GIs pressed forward from the beach and established a firing line on the edge of the jungle. On Blue Beach the 321st met stiffer resistance: enemy fortified positions on their flanks at Rockey Point to the south and Cape Ngatpokul to the north slowed them down, and by nightfall on the 17th they held only a precarious foothold about 1,500 yards long and penetrating 500 yards into the thick undergrowth.

From Red Beach the 322nd RCT pushed rapidly inland, and so good was their progress that they were given the go-ahead to attempt to reach the objective set for D+1. By early evening on the 17th they were almost half-way across the island, but there was still a dangerous 700-yard gap between their left flank and the 321st. With the darkness, inevitably, came the Japanese counter-attacks.

The Army troops, in action for the first time, were understandably 'trigger-happy', and Maj. Goto's men were quick to probe the American lines for any weaknesses. The 1st Battalion of the 321st were particularly hard pressed, and had to withdraw 75 yards until their line was stabilised. 'A lot happened that first night. As it got dark we took turns watching the enemy [while] the other three would take off their helmets and try to sleep, [but] no one had told us about the land crabs', says Tom Climie. 'They are hard-shelled and about the size of a pretty good dinner plate. When the first one fell into the foxhole and fell on to a helmet, you can imagine the noise – four men jumped up and had their rifles and bayonets ready . . .

'While I was on watch, there was a bush in the distance and a light breeze blowing it, at times it looked like a Jap creeping up – I had my rifle with the safety off trained on it for two hours.

'We heard some cans rattling and everybody fired at it; I looked and saw a dog running with his tail wagging, I think he got through unhit.'

* * *

The morning of 18 September brought carrier planes to strafe the enemy directly in front of the precarious Army front, and with the support of artillery and Sherman tanks both RCTs were soon on the move again.

The 322nd pushed westward, only slowing when they reached the high ground in the centre of Angaur, and by 2.00pm they had reached the phosphate plant a few hundred yards north-east of Saipan Town. It was during this advance that a tragic blunder occurred. Responding to incorrect information, a number of carrier planes bombed and strafed units of the 3/322nd, killing seven men of the battalion and wounding 46 others.

Pushing inland from Blue Beach, the 321st finally established contact with the 322nd and closed the gap between them. The advanced elements pushed on to the west, while the 1/321st swung to the south. The battalion soon came upon the fortifications that Maj. Goto had constructed around Green Beaches 2 & 3 – a complex system of field works which stretched for some 1,500 yards. Colonel Dark's GIs had the advantage that most of the positions faced seaward in anticipation of the landings that had never materialised; however, dense jungle and an area of swampland frustrated any chance of an immediate attack, and a long wait ensued until tanks and other supporting weapons could be brought up.

The third day saw Angaur cut in two on a broad front, with the Japanese isolated into three pockets: one was the area around the Green Beaches, another was at the southern tip of the island, while the third – and by far the largest – was around Ramuldo Hill in the north-west corner of the island.

* * *

The Green Beach defences and the southern pocket fell on D+3, 20 September, and Gen. Mueller signalled Roy Geiger aboard the *Mount McKinley*: 'As of 1034hrs this date, target has been secured'. However, it was up north in the Ramuldo Hill area that Maj. Goto of the 59th Infantry had decided to make his last stand. With his 700 remaining men – twice the number that Gen. Mueller had estimated – he was to hold out not for a few days, but for a full month, until 22 October.

These premature announcements of victory were to be an occasional feature of the Pacific campaigns. On Iwo Jima, Gen. Harry Schmidt would hold a flag-raising ceremony to declare the island 'secure' on 14 March 1945, only to have the staff officer's speech drowned out by the gunfire in the north of the island; the 3rd, 4th and 5th Marine Divisions had to fight on for another 14 days before they suppressed the last active units of Gen. Kuribayashi's fanatical defenders. Such misjudgements were not as vainglorious as they may seem in retrospect, but were sometimes due to a basic misunderstanding of the Japanese psyche – to any Western professional soldier, the point at which they announced victory was the point at which any further enemy resistance would have seemed insane.

So the 322nd RCT were to be occupied for another four weeks winkling Goto's defenders out of the maze of natural and man-made caves around Ramuldo Hill. Dug in with mortars, machine guns and a few pieces of artillery, they survived air attacks and naval bombardments. It was left to Col. Venable's GIs to employ the resources that would ultimately secure the Umurbrogol hills on Peleliu: demolition charges, grenades, flamethrowers, small arms, and the sheer guts of the fighting infantry.

General Geiger signalled Mueller to retain the 322nd on Angaur until all resistance had ceased, and to deploy the divisional reserve, the 323rd RCT, to the Ulithi Attack Group. This force, under Adm. Blandy, comprised a powerful fleet of carriers, battleships, cruisers and destroyers. They arrived at Ulithi the following day and occupied the atoll without firing a shot. Thought by the Navy to be a heavily defended base, Ulithi was empty of any Japanese troops. With its excellent natural harbour, it soon became one of the main staging areas for later Navy and Marine operations during the relentless drive towards the Japanese homeland.

On 19 October, Maj. Ushio Goto was finally killed, and three days later the last enemy position on Angaur was overrun. The operation had cost the 81st Division 260 men killed and 1,354 wounded, with a further 940 incapacitated by disease or unspecified causes. The Japanese casualties were estimated at 1,338 killed; just 59 were taken prisoner.

Even before the suppression of the Ramuldo pocket the Seabees and 81st Division engineers had cleared the jungle and scrubland for the airfield that was eventually to dominate the island, but it was never to be used for the purpose for which it had been intended, to support the advance through the Philippines. The airfield became operational on 15 October, and by November B-24 Liberator bombers of the 494th Bomb Group were flying from Angaur.

* * *

In 1995, Tom Climie of the 321st RCT and his wife Shirley decided that Angaur should have a war memorial. Peleliu had several – Army, Marine and Japanese – but there was nothing to commemorate the 81st Division's campaign on Angaur. Extensive enquiries among 'Wildcat' associations failed to raise a cent, however; so they decided to finance the venture themselves. They had a plaque made at their own expense; the Governor of Angaur provided a site near Blue Beach, and the Seabees built a plinth and attached the plaque to it.

'Shirley and I went over in December 1995, and we had a great ceremony dedicating this beautiful monument', wrote Tom. 'In the year since the dedication, the Royal Belau Yacht Club, made up of Americans who have lived in the Palaus for ten to fifteen years, have planted grass, flowers and shrubs around the monument, placed poles and put a chain from pole to pole, and painted it all white. They claim that it is now the prettiest monument anywhere in the Pacific.'

CHAPTER 10

Bloody Nose Ridge

The morning of 17 September – D+2 – found the Marines holding a firm line across the island just north of the airfield. Ahead lay the Umurbrogol 'Mountains' edged by the East and West Roads. In the south, Ngarmoked Island and parts of the south-east promontory were still in enemy hands, but the 7th Regiment were preparing for what they hoped would be the final clearance of this area.

The Japanese had already suffered heavy casualties and many pillboxes, weapon emplacements and blockhouses had been destroyed or overrun; but the bulk of the defenders were now taking up their positions in the Umurbrogol, in the warren of caves that Col. Nakagawa had chosen and prepared as the site for his last battle.

Marine casualties had also been heavy: the 1st Regiment alone had suffered nearly 1,000 dead and wounded in just two days. Moreover, the heat and shortage of clean water had had a serious impact on the troops' fighting efficiency. Eventually the engineers would dig ground wells and install distillation units which would provide 50,000 gallons of water a day; but until then the merciless sun blasting down on the rocks of Peleliu would seem to be fighting on the side of the soldiers who marched beneath its flag.

* * *

As the morning temperature spiralled, the 7th Regiment moved out from its overnight positions. Sergeant Jim Moll of Company A, 1/7th, recalls:

'To get to Ngarmoked Island there was a causeway about 100 yards long; at the end of the causeway was a large blockhouse, and off on the sides some pillboxes to lay down heavy machine gun fire. Companies B and C tried to cross but couldn't make it – they both had many casualties; so Able was next. The whole causeway was littered with wounded and dead Marines . . . I ran at full speed, [but] about half way across I recognised this young Marine that I knew as "Jersey Joe" – I was from New Jersey, and this young Marine, who was no more than sixteen, used to chat to me about Jersey. When he saw me he yelled, "Sarge, help me!"

'I was already past him but I came back; his helmet was off and the young guy's leg was shot off just above the knee and still attached to the body by a piece of the thigh, and blood was pouring out. I took his trouser belt off to use as a tourniquet, yelled for a Corpsman a couple of times, and wished him good luck. I shall never forget that kid if I live to be a hundred.'

Company A had attacked at 2.30pm after a ten-minute air strike and with the support of three Shermans. The first line of the Japanese defences was penetrated; now began the grim business of slugging it out with the entrenched enemy, yard by yard.

* * *

The south-eastern promontory, a shallow triangle joined to the rest of the island by a narrow neck, looked the more vulnerable of the two remaining enemy outposts on the southern tip of the island. It was known that there were fewer Japanese here, and the terrain did not offer them the cover of the hills and rocky outcrops that dominated Ngarmoked Island. The initial attack had to be postponed for two hours while the 1st Engineers, under covering fire, cleared a minefield on the neck leading to the promontory. Once this task was completed, however, the Marines, supported by their Shermans, swarmed over the sand spit; and by 1.30pm the remaining Japanese were taking to the water in a vain attempt to cross over to Ngarmoked Island. From vantage points on the shoreline the Marines shot them down one by one, like targets in a fairground booth.

Correspondent Tom Lea accompanied a patrol heading for the promontory: 'As the sun climbed in the clear sky the heat grew, there was no breeze and stinging sweat poured from our bodies and kept us wet in our muddy dungarees. That morning Marines learned the full force of the sun on Peleliu, where coral rock bakes in the oven of the sky. The heat cut into our very marrow as we trudged along the ridge; the dead Japs were also affected by the heat, they had started to stink before they were stiff. Over in some dry grass by a tree I stood a moment looking down at the face of a dead Marine – he seemed so quiet and empty and past all the small things a man could love or hate.'

The Japanese had spent a considerable amount of time preparing their defensive positions on Ngarmoked Island. The terrain was favourable, with high ground to the north, opposite the Unnamed Island, and in the extreme south. The Marines concentrated their firepower – artillery, mortars and tanks – on these two areas, and Navy planes provided excellent air support.

Colonel Hanneken realised at around dusk that he had little chance of clearing the island on D+2, and broke off the fighting to establish his defence line for the night. The Japanese were content to remain in their prepared positions, and the Marines had a rare incident-free night. James Moll takes up his story on the morning of 18 September – D+3:

'Early the next morning, I was enjoying a cup of joe [coffee] with Shanahan, which was one of those fantastic K-rations. The hot sun was coming up, and with the heat the flies started swarming all over the bloated, stinking dead Jap soldiers who were lying all over the place. The flies were so bad it was hard to keep them out of your joe, so you had to keep your free hand waving over your cup at all times . . . Oh boy! The stench got worse every minute.

'Three strange Marines came along looking all over the area; one was elderly, the other two were young, their clothes were clean and you knew they weren't any of the grunts . . . One of the young guys approached me and Shanahan and asked who the hell was in charge. I said I carried the rank of sergeant if that was any help, so this Marine – without introducing himself – told me to get some men and start burying the stinking dead Japs. I told him we only kill them, someone else has to bury them. The elderly guy looked our way and said, 'Lieutenant, you better not disturb these guys while they're having their breakfast', and they took off. Later we found out that the elderly guy was Colonel Hanneken, our regimental commander.'

Reinforcements of tanks and men, freed up from the occupation of the south-eastern promontory, were ready by 10.00am, and the final phase of the assault on Ngarmoked began. Half-way down the peninsula lay a swamp; the plan for the day was for Companies A and C of the 1/7th Marines to circle around it and tie up in line to drive to the south.

It took three hours of hard fighting under the broiling sun for Company B, who had been committed on the left, to reach the southern shore. This left the western area, with its mass of rocks, trenches and foxholes, to Companies A and C.

During the relentless advance many Japanese positions were overrun, and it became necessary to commit the reserve units – Company I of the 3/7th, and the division's Reconnaissance Company – to deal with the unexpectedly large number of enemy troops who swarmed out from these positions.

The Japanese had always anticipated a Marine landing in the cove that separated Ngarmoked Island from the south-east promontory, and had arranged their defences accordingly. The beaches were all heavily mined and a chain of blockhouses, pillboxes and gun emplacements covered all approaches to the cove. Although most of these defences faced seaward, suppressing them still proved difficult. By 2.00pm on 18 September the Marines estimated that they had killed about 350 of the enemy and that the remainder had been squeezed into a pocket of approximately 150 square yards.

As the Marines waited for their tanks to re-arm and for a bulldozer to extricate bogged-down halftracks – which mounted 75mm anti-tank guns in the regimental weapons companies – shots were heard coming from the enemy fortifications and men were seen jumping into the sea. The Japanese, realising the hopelessness of their situation, were committing mass suicide. Colonel Hanneken called the divisional CP at 3.20pm and informed Gen. Rupertus that the 7th Regiment had completed their mission. As far as could be calculated, 2,609 Japanese had died in southern Peleliu; there were no prisoners – an ominous portent for the rest of the battle. The 7th Marines had lost 27 dead, 414 wounded and 36 missing. The 'brass' were very concerned: the south had been regarded as the easy part of the operation.

* * *

With the drive to secure the south well underway, Gen. Rupertus concentrated on driving north into the Umurbrogol, and east to the village of Ngardololok, where the Japanese had a radio direction finder station (see Map 3, page 52 – 'RDF').

After their murderous advance across the flat expanse of the airfield, the 5th Regiment had been engaged in bitter exchanges with diehard defenders among the rubble of the Japanese HQ and barracks area which lay between the east–west runway and the foothills of the Umurbrogol. On 17 September, D+2, the regiment moved forward, with the 1/5th on the left and the 2/5th on the right. The 1st Battalion had borne the brunt of the previous day's fighting, and it was decided to relieve them with the 3rd Battalion. Despite coming under heavy enemy fire from the Japanese positions in the Umurbrogol foothills, the exchange was completed by 12.30pm.

The 2nd Battalion swung to the east among the heavily wooded approaches to the village of Omaok, and found the enemy resistance to be minimal. Nevertheless, there were still bursts of artillery fire coming from the hills whenever the Americans were observed by the enemy spotters – an attempt to supplement the advance with a Sherman tank brought down such a volume of fire that it had to make a hasty withdrawal.

By noon the heat peaked somewhere near 110°F, and the troops were forced to make frequent stops to rest and to wait for water to be brought forward. What was marked on the maps as the village of Omaok proved to be a rubble of demolished barracks and outbuildings, and the 2/5th dug in for the night on the outskirts. John C.Brewer, a heavy equipment operator with the 1st Engineer Battalion, was meanwhile attempting to construct some roads in the area that the 5th Regiment had captured to the east of the airfield:

'I cleaned up the area so that our little friends would have a harder time pulling a sneak attack. I started pioneering a road up the other side of the airfield; undergrowth was pretty thick there and it wasn't easy to see what was in there. Sometimes I would get a dead Jap – if I didn't get all of him the first time I would scatter guts the whole width of the road and get the rest of him on the next pass. Human bodies deteriorate fast in the tropics. One whiff of a dead Jap at bed time meant no sleep, that is the worst smell I have ever smelled.' Human dignity and the niceties of burial had little value on a Pacific battlefield.

* * *

Aided by a half-hour barrage of artillery fire, the 2/5th Marines made an early 7.00am start the following day, D+3, and brushed aside feeble resistance to reach the road connecting Omaok and Ngardololok within two hours. Beyond here the land narrowed to a 200-foot-wide neck connecting with the eastern mass of forest and mangrove swamp to the rear of the coastal strip defined on the Marines' maps as Purple Beach.

The Japanese made a major tactical error in not reinforcing this natural causeway, which could have been a serious bottleneck for the Marines. It was known that the enemy had defensive installations at the RDF site and in the vicinity of Purple Beach, so it seemed incomprehensible that the causeway would not also be heavily defended. With the prospect of strong resistance around Ngardololok and the RDF, an air strike was requested to soften up the defences. It was here that one of the blunders that inevitably accompany most battles occurred.

The carrier planes missed Ngardololok altogether, so an artillery barrage from the 11th Marine Artillery was substituted, set for 1.35pm. The 2nd Battalion's Companies F and G then commenced the crossing of the causeway – only to be bombed and strafed by a totally unexpected and uncalled-for second air strike. To add to the chaos, Company E and the 2/5th's battalion command post, moving forward in support, were blasted by misdirected Marine artillery and mortar fire. These incidents of 'friendly fire' were responsible for the deaths of 18 of the 2nd Battalion's Marines.

On the evening of D+3 the battalion dug in on a line from north to south facing the main Ngardololok installations across an area of open ground (see Map 6, page 114). Machine-gunner Jim Johnston could still maintain his sense of humour:

'On the beach near Ngardololok there were signs of recent habitation. On the floor of one of the huts I found a heap of loose rice that I put to good use. I filled my canteen cup about half full of water and shaved some of my D-ration (chocolate) into it, then I added the Jap rice to the mixture and built a fire and heated it all. Before I finished eating it I noticed some of the rice moving – on closer inspection I found that quite a large part of the rice pile was maggots. That was one helluva chocolate pudding.'

The 2/5th Marines' attack on the RDF and Ngardololok village on 19 September, D+4, proved to be something of an anti-climax. Another air strike paved the way for the occupation of the village, but only scattered resistance was encountered, leading to the suspicion that the enemy had virtually abandoned the whole area. Subsequent operations that day

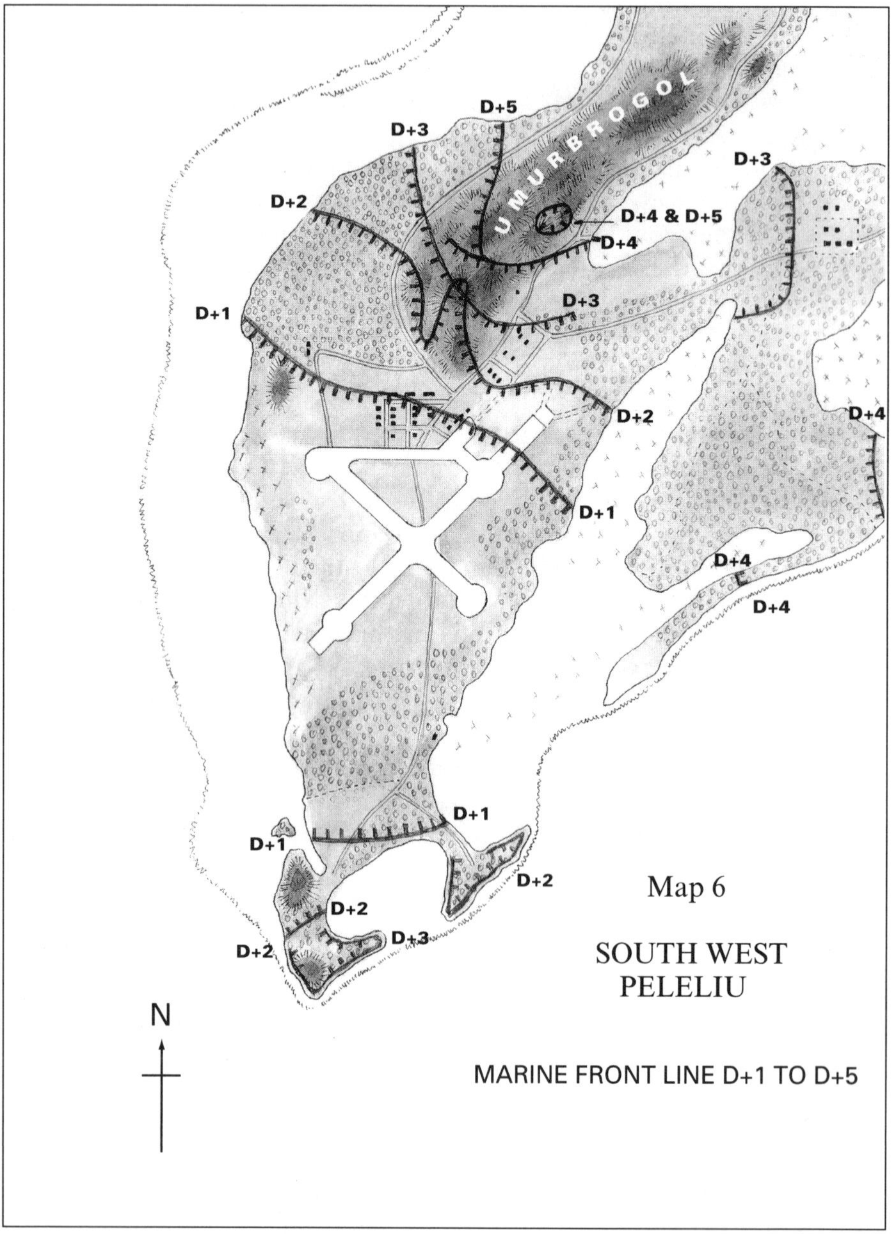
UMURBROGOL
D+5
D+3
D+2
D+1
D+4 & D+5
D+4
D+3
D+3
D+2
D+1
D+4
D+4
D+4
D+1
D+1
D+2
D+2
D+3
D+2
N
Map 6
SOUTH WEST
PELELIU
MARINE FRONT LINE D+1 TO D+5

confirmed the supposition as the Marines steadily moved towards Purple Beach, which was reached that evening.

An inspection of the defences in this area confirmed the wisdom of siting the invasion to the west of the airfield. The whole beach was heavily mined and strewn with anti-tank obstructions, and was backed by a dense complex of barricades and pillboxes. Mopping up continued throughout the day, and on the 20th, D+5, the Purple Beach area was in American hands. Patrols sailed out to the offshore islands and occupied Island 'A' and Ngabad Island (see Map 2, page 51), both of which were unoccupied; and on the 23rd they secured the abandoned unnamed island which lay offshore south-east from Radar Hill in the north of Peleliu.

All that remained was the narrow tongue of land stretching south-west from Purple Beach, which was allocated to Company I of the 3/5th Regiment. Here the few remaining Japanese had organised an ambush for the approaching Marines, but were foiled by an alert war dog whose actions no doubt saved many lives.

'On the fourth day we were moved to another position on the island – Purple Beach, where we set up a defence line against any infiltration from the high ground or from the water,' recalls Sterling Mace of the 5th Regiment. 'The next morning our company made another move. This time the deployment carried us past a mangrove swamp; knee-deep in water we made our way through the brush and vegetation – then came the explosion. Branches and stems of trees shattered into fragments, the water and mud flew high in the air – whether it was a booby trap or a tossed hand grenade we never found out. Levy took its force in his face – it was what is called a "million dollar wound"; he was hit in the chin. Bloody and wrapped in gauze, Levy was evacuated to a hospital ship; he was seventeen years old, a kid from Brooklyn – I thought I'd never see him again.'

Well away from the battle that was starting in the Umurbrogol upland, this eastern side of Peleliu became a 'defence area', to be occupied successively by an assortment of units who were relieved from the front line for short periods of rest.

* * *

Place names on Peleliu were always a problem for the Marines; Ngardololok, Ngesebus, Ngarmoked and Kamilianiui were tongue-twisters for the average Leatherneck, so when they came up against the Umurbrogol they coined their own name – 'Bloody Nose Ridge'. Highly appropriate in its simplicity, the name became synonymous with some of the most horrific fighting of the entire Pacific campaign.

The narrative of the 1st Regiment describes the terrain: 'The ground of Peleliu's western peninsula was the worst ever encountered by the

Regiment in three Pacific campaigns. Along its centre, the rocky spine was heaped up in a contorted mass of decaying coral, strewn with rubble, crags, ridges and gulches thrown together in a confusing maze. There were no roads, scarcely any trails, the pock-marked surface offered no secure footing even in the few level places. It was impossible to dig in, the best the men could do was to pile a little coral or wood debris around their positions; the jagged rock slashed their boots and clothes, and tore their bodies every time they hit the deck for safety.

'Casualties were higher for the simple reason [that] it was impossible to get under the ground away from the Japanese mortar barrage; each blast hurtled chunks of coral in all directions, multiplying many times the fragmentation effect of every shell. Into this the enemy dug and tunnelled like moles, and there they stayed to fight to the death.'

In a post-war personal narrative Gen. Oliver Smith gave his impression of the Umurbrogol: 'Ravines, which on the maps and photographs appeared to be steep-sided, actually had sheer cliffs for sides, some of them 50–100 feet high. With nothing else on your mind but to cover the distance between two points, walking was difficult . . . There were dozens of caves and pillboxes worked into the nose of the ridges and up the ravines, it was very difficult to find blind spots as the caves and pillboxes were mutually supporting . . . These caves and pillboxes housed riflemen, machine gunners, mortars, rockets and field pieces. The Japanese technique was to run the piece out of the cave, fire, then run the piece back into the cave before we could react.'

Colonel Puller's 1st Regiment had taken a mauling from the outset of the landings, with the 3/1st suffering heavy casualties from the coral ridge facing White Beach 1, and Capt. Hunt's bloody battle at The Point; the total casualty list so far, exceeding 1,000, did not include men suffering from heat exhaustion and battle fatigue. On 17 September – D+2 – 'Chesty' contacted Col. Selden, the divisional chief of staff, on the field telephone:

'Johnny, half my regiment is gone, I've got to have replacements to carry out division orders tomorrow morning.'

'You know we have no replacements, Lewie,' was the reply.

Puller stormed, 'I told you before we came ashore that we should have at least one regiment in reserve! We're not fighting [i.e. employing in the front line] a third of the men we brought in – all those damn specialists you brought.'

'Anything wrong with your orders, Lewie?', asked Selden.

'No, I'm ready to go ahead, but you know my casualties are 50 per cent now,' said Puller.

'What do you want me to do?', yelled Selden.

'Give me some of those 1,700 men on the beach,' retorted Puller.

'You can't have them – they're not trained infantry.'

'Give 'em to me, and by nightfall tomorrow they'll be trained infantry.' At that point Selden hung up on Puller.

The 2nd Battalion of the 7th Regiment, the divisional reserve who had been sent from their ship to the reef and back again on D-Day, had finally got ashore by late on D+1 and had already been assigned to 'Chesty' Puller; they were soon to play an active part in the fighting. Meanwhile his 1st Battalion, under Maj. Ray Davis, had come across an unexpected obstacle, a blockhouse with 4-foot-thick reinforced concrete walls and surrounded by at least 12 pillboxes. This formidable structure had shown clearly on the pre-invasion aerial photographs, and should have been destroyed by the fire support ships – so much for Adm. Oldendorf's comment that he had run out of worthwhile targets. On D+2, fire control soon had the battleship *Mississippi*'s 14in guns homed in on the target, and the blockhouse disintegrated under a storm of armour-piercing shells. Tanks and infantry suppressed the adjacent pillboxes. Major Davis – later to become a general and Korean War Medal of Honor winner – recalls:

'In my sector a short distance inland we came face to face with a gigantic blockhouse, walls of concrete several feet thick; it had not been nicked at all, even though it was listed on the target list. We were stalled until the battleship *Mississippi* attacked it with 14in shells, [but] we also had to knock out pillboxes and bunkers nearby – 35 of my Marines were killed or wounded in this assault.'

* * *

The first Marines to go up against Bloody Nose Ridge on D+2 were Lt.Col. Honsowetz's 2nd Battalion of Puller's 1st Regiment. In the wake of a naval and artillery bombardment they overran the section where the East and West Roads joined, and advanced for about 150 yards before encountering intense fire from a coral ridge to their left. With its sheer flanks riddled with caves, this Hill 200 – named after its elevation above sea level – not only pinned down Honsowetz's men but afforded the Japanese a commanding overview of the airfield and the invasion beaches to the west.

Moving to the left, the 2/1st Marines began an all-out assault in the face of devastating enemy fire; as one position was silenced, the same gunner would appear from another one only yards away. It was becoming obvious that the Japanese were very well prepared, and that the pre-invasion maps and intelligence reports about the Umurbrogol were grossly inaccurate.

Shermans and LVT(A) Amtanks were rushed forward in support, but at such close range they too were knocked out left and right and were forced to retire. Marine artillery and the Navy's big guns were directed at Hill 200 and succeeded in reducing the volume of enemy fire slightly, but the hard work was left to the troops on the ground. Crawling and slithering across diamond-sharp outcrops of coral, seeking any cover that was available, they suffered a constant hail of mortar, artillery and small arms fire from the heights above. Further to the right, Maj. Ray Davis's 1st Battalion were now facing the ridges too:

'The men surged forward again, slugging their way upward much in the manner of the 2nd Battalion, there was no other way – clawing up and over razor-back crests, shinnying coral pinnacles, plunging down into sheer-sided gullies and ravines, dodging behind boulders.'

Casualties in both battalions mounted fast as Marines fell under shredding enemy fire and collapsed from the 110°-plus heat. By early evening, Davis and his men had established themselves among the forward slopes of the ridges and had accounted for over 35 enemy caves. From the rear, engineers and anyone else who could be pressed into service found themselves donning combat gear and moving forward to bolster the ever-thinning ranks on the front line.

By nightfall, Honsowetz and his 2nd Battalion had slugged their way to the summit of Hill 200, but casualties had been severe. From their left flank heavy fire from another hill – 10 feet higher in elevation and thus called Hill 210 – forced them down behind whatever cover was available to suffer in silence. Exploiting a gap between the 1st and 2nd Battalions, the Japanese began to infiltrate, and a company of the 7th Regiment had to be brought forward to plug the gap. The Japanese continued to harry the Marines throughout the night. Marine rifleman John Brewer remembers:

'We had strung trip wires around the periphery of the area and put cans on the wires. We used C-ration cans that we had punched holes in with our bayonets. During the night the cans started rattling and we started throwing hand grenades; we also called out the number of our foxhole – [after] about the fifth number called, some character down the line hollered out "Bingo!" – how can you whip that kind of humour?

'At daylight we went out to see how many Japs we had killed. We had gotten a wild sow and her piglets . . . we had pork and shrapnel for breakfast.'

The mortar fire during the night was particularly fierce. Fired at a high angle, mortar bombs descend almost vertically, and there is no hiding from them. R.Bruce Watkins of the 2/1st remembers one of his men who suffered the effects of the mortar barrage that night:

'About midnight I heard a call for help about five yards to my left front. Even with good fire discipline it was difficult to move at night without getting shot by your own men – I yelled ahead and repeated the password several times while crawling forward. When I got there I discovered it was

Pfc. Buckey Buckner, and he had taken a fatal wound in the abdomen from a mortar fragment. By the light of almost constant flares I could see that there was little hope, his stomach was in ruins. I called for a Corpsman and one of those brave Navy men crawled up to help. He, too, knew it was useless, but since Buckey was conscious and in pain he got out a morphine syrette and gave him a shot. Left alone, Buckey and I talked as I lay beside him in the foxhole; he was very young, about twenty, and had a wife and a baby, and naturally they were uppermost in his mind. As his pain got worse I gave him more morphine; for perhaps two hours he drifted in and out of consciousness, [until] finally he was still – I just hoped that my hand on his was a little comfort towards the end.'

To the west, Lt.Col. Sabol's 3rd Battalion were advancing along the relatively flat coastal strip parallel to the Umurbrogol; they only halted after an advance of 700 yards because they were afraid they might over-extend the line. By nightfall on D+2 the front resembled a rough letter W (see Map 6, page 114): in the centre the 2nd Battalion were well forward with their occupation of Hill 200, while on their left flank the Japanese held Hill 210, which formed a salient into the American positions.

Unknown to the Marines, they had come within a short distance of Col. Nakagawa's command post, and the Japanese commander had to relocate his HQ as it was becoming too vulnerable. The Marines were later to discover this position, which was complete with electricity and other amenities, and extended through the full width of the ridge in which it was sited.

* * *

The fourth day of the battle, 18 September, was to prove almost catastrophic for the 1st Marines.

Since D-Day they had now taken 1,236 casualties, and although boosted by replacements from headquarters units – dog handlers, engineers, anyone who could handle a rifle – the regiment's fighting efficiency was nearing rock bottom. The 1st Battalion had had to be withdrawn from the line for a while, and the 2nd Battalion of the 7th Regiment relieved it under Puller's command.

The now-standard bombardment by naval guns, artillery and carrier planes began at 7.00am on D+3, after which the 3rd Battalion made a further advance along the western coastal strip against light resistance, halting after a quarter of a mile in order not to lose contact with the 2nd Battalion on their right. It was in the centre, on Bloody Nose Ridge, that the day's bitterest fighting was to occur.

Driving the enemy from Hill 210 and gaining the ground beyond Hill 200 were the prime objectives. Desperate fighting ensued, with the

Japanese responding with mortars, machine guns, rockets, and well-concealed large-calibre artillery. As the Marines gradually drove the enemy from Hill 210, they retaliated by mounting a major counter-attack against Hill 200 which forced a temporary American retreat. By 2.00pm the 2nd Battalion's Lt.Col. Honsowetz was desperately calling his regimental commander on the field telephone to tell him that the situation was becoming critical. Puller's reply was typical: 'Goddammit, you get those troops in there and you take that hill!'

With a few reinforcements and the help of a smokescreen, Honsowetz's men took Hill 205 slightly to the side of Hill 210, but this proved to be useful only as an observation point. In trying to move further forward, the battalion came across yet another formidable line of defensive positions subsequently to be named 'Five Sisters'.

Another Medal of Honor was to be won that day. Private First Class Charles Roan, from the town of Claude in the Texas Panhandle, was with four other Marines from the 2/7th when they found themselves cut off and fighting a grenade duel with Japanese in a nearby cave. Wounded by a nearby explosion, Roan suddenly saw a well-aimed grenade land in the middle of his group; without a thought for his own safety, he covered the grenade with his body and died instantly in the blast – his four companions were later to escape when a tank bulldozer arrived on the scene half an hour later.

Evening revealed only minor gains, and on Hill 200 there had actually been the loss of a small area; casualties had been appalling, and Puller was in a sombre mood.

* * *

'All infantry units will resume the attack with maximum effort in all sectors at 0830hrs on September 19th' – thus read Gen. Rupertus' order of the day. He appears to have been more than a little out of touch with the plight of the 1st Regiment, and could only see his prediction of a three-day battle being exposed as the nonsense that most of his staff had always regarded it. Reduced to throwing into the fighting line cooks, clerks, military police, laundry workers, dog handlers, drivers, and the non-combatant black troops who usually handled ammunition and supplies, 'Chesty' Puller was desperately trying to implement the general's orders.

D+4 started much the same as the previous day; artillery and heavy fire from the battleships offshore heralded an attack across the whole northern front. Again the 3rd Battalion of the 1st Regiment made the most significant gains, advancing another 400 yards along the coast before being forced to halt in order to maintain contact.

In the centre, the Marines were beginning to appreciate the true nature of the Five Sisters. Their maps showed the area as a series of interconnecting hillocks; in reality the Sisters were a wall that barred any progress northward. Far from being connected, the five hills were separated by precipitous ravines, and the southern face from which the Marines were forced to make their assault was almost sheer – even if they could capture one of the Sisters, there was no way that they could move directly to the next one.

As many heavy weapons as possible were brought forward that day – tanks, bazookas, mortars, heavy machine guns, and both man-portable and self-propelled flame throwers – the latter being three modified LVT-4 Amtracs. All proved of little avail; and as the casualties mounted the 1st Marines continued to dwindle before their commander's eyes. Company A, back from the 1/1st's short break from battle, passed through elements of the 7th Regiment. The company had just 56 men at the start of the day; struggling to secure a small area of high ground, they found themselves decimated by Japanese machine gun fire but doggedly pressed on, only to be confronted by a sheer 150-foot drop that was conspicuously absent from their field maps. Cursing the deskbound planners, they painfully began to extricate themselves amid a hail of enemy fire: only six men returned to the 7th Regiment lines unscathed. By afternoon, Russell Honsowetz had committed all his rifle companies to the line and there were no reserves.

In an attempt to break the deadlock, Honsowetz had earlier committed what was left of Company C of the 1st Battalion in a manoeuvre designed to outflank the Five Sisters. To the left of the East Road and to the rear of the Sisters lay Hill 100. If this could be taken it might provide an opening to the rear of the enemy. Commanded by Capt. Everett Pope, the 90-man company – all that remained of the 242 officers and men who had landed on D-Day – began their hazardous advance. The direct approach to the base of Hill 100 was through a small mangrove swamp, but almost at once they were pinned down by machine gun fire from two pillboxes about 500 yards ahead. Pope's men stayed where they were for almost two hours while he discussed the options with Honsowetz and awaited the arrival of tank support. Further along the East Road the swamp could be crossed by a narrow causeway across the mouth of a wide valley later to be named the Horseshoe; once across, the Marines could skirt the base of Hill 100.

However, things were not destined to go Pope's way that day. The first of the Shermans attempted to cross the causeway but slithered over the side and became bogged down; a second tank moved forward to attempt to pull it out, and immediately slid over the other side, blocking the way. Faced with the choice of attempting to clear both tanks, or making a mad dash across the causeway on foot, Pope elected the latter. His men rushed across by squads, catching the enemy by surprise and without sustaining any casualties. After a brief regrouping, between 25 and 30 Marines charged the slopes of Hill 100 supported by mortar and machine gun fire from a group which remained on the far side of the swamp to provide a base of fire, and with astonishing ease they reached the summit. Only then were they to realize that they too had fallen foul of the map makers: Hill 100 was not an isolated summit, as indicated, but merely the southern nose of a long ridge – later named 'Walt Ridge' – and dominated by a higher position only 500 yards to their front (see Map 8, page 143).

Evening was now approaching and Pope's options had run out; they were surrounded, and with no hope of reinforcement before dawn they were looking at a grim night. The men of Charlie Company did not have long to wait; from almost point blank range the enemy poured mortar and machine gun fire on to the besieged Marines, and at around 5.00pm infantry began to infiltrate the American positions. Japanese soldiers excelled in night-fighting and the trickery that went with it; they were taught to call out a few words of English so as to tempt defenders into revealing their positions – often mimicking a wounded man's cry for a medic, or using common names like Bill or Joe. At first in small groups, and later in bands of 20 to 25, they tried to dislodge the Marines, who fought them off in a series of bitter hand-to-hand engagements. Lightly armed with only a few machine guns and a limited number of grenades, the men of Company C soon found their ammunition running out, and were eventually reduced to fighting for their lives with knives, stones, empty ammunition boxes and bare fists. By dawn there were only 15 men and one officer left.

The order came through for the survivors to evacuate, just as the Japanese were mounting an assault that would inevitably have swept the Marines off the hill. Scrambling down under cover of a smoke screen and artillery fire, Pope and his men dodged a barrage of mortar bombs unleashed by the enemy above, and finally reached the cover of a stone wall near the causeway. Over two dozen men had gone up Hill 100 on the previous day; only nine were to return and of these many, including Capt. Pope, were wounded.

At 4.30pm on D+5, while the survivors were nursing their wounds, orders came through for Company C to attack along a ravine near Hill 100. When Pope reported that his company consisted of 15 unwounded men and two officers, the order was rescinded. Captain Pope was later awarded the Medal of Honor for the action on Hill 100, and four of his men received the Navy Cross, the Marine Corps' second highest decoration.

* * *

Reinforcements were sorely needed to replace the shattered 1st Regiment, and they were readily available – from the Army's 81st Division on Angaur; but Gen. Rupertus was bitterly opposed to their use. Inter-service rivalries are common among the armed forces of all countries, but the reluctance of Gen. Rupertus to accept the help of the Army on Peleliu had its origins in a particularly vitriolic episode which clouded the relationship of the USMC and the US Army during the Pacific War.

During Operation Galvanic in November 1943, when the 2nd Marine Division made their shockingly bloody assault on the tiny island of Betio at Tarawa Atoll, the occupation of the more northerly island of Makin was entrusted to the Army's 27th Infantry Division, commanded by Maj.Gen. Ralph Smith. The Marines, in a now-famous battle, occupied Betio in 76 hours of some of the costliest fighting of the war; but on Makin the 6,500 Army troops, who were fighting a mere 800 Japanese defenders, were so lethargic that the Marine Commander of V Amphibious Corps, Maj.Gen. Holland Smith, made a personal appearance on the island to investigate. When told that there was heavy opposition in the north of the island, he commandeered a jeep and went to see for himself, only to find the area 'as quiet as Wall Street on a Sunday'. Living up to his nickname of 'Howlin' Mad', Smith castigated his Army namesake over the three days that it took to occupy the island.

The 'Smith vs Smith' feud reached its climax during the invasion of Saipan in 1944. When the 27th Division's advance bogged down, leaving gaps on the flanks of the 2nd and 4th Marine Divisions who were surging ahead, 'Howlin' Mad' Smith relieved Ralph Smith of his command for 'lack of aggressiveness'. This incident caused a deep antagonism between some members of the Army and the Marine Corps that was to last until the end of the war and beyond, and which would have serious consequences for Holland Smith. Senior Army staff at the Pentagon were soon sharpening their knives; and a group of influential newspaper tycoons, headed by Randolph Hearst, seized upon the incident to fuel their anti-Marine and pro-MacArthur campaign, which was directed at promoting Gen. Douglas MacArthur as the next President. Even the usually placid Nimitz turned against Holland Smith, and he was not invited to attend the Japanese surrender ceremony aboard the USS *Missouri* in Tokyo Bay – a gesture that he took more as an insult to his Marines than as a personal rebuff (although Gen. Roy Geiger was there to represent the Corps).

To what extent Rupertus was influenced by this inter-service wrangling is unclear; what is certain is that he was to press his men so hard that they were in danger of being annihilated, and that it took the direct intervention of Roy Geiger to force him to accept the assistance of the Army GIs of Mueller's 81st Division on Peleliu.

* * *

In the meantime, the ever-determined 'Chesty' Puller believed that one more concerted effort by his Marines on 20 September – D+5 – could achieve the much-needed breakthrough. His efforts were concentrated on Walt Ridge, the area immediately north of Hill 100 where Pope and his men had struggled so gallantly the previous day. Employing anyone who could be put into the line, the attack inevitably floundered as the exhausted troops battled against an enemy deeply dug into almost unassailable positions. The assault on Walt Ridge that day signalled the end of the 1st Regiment as an effective fighting unit; Col. Puller would not admit the fact, nor would Gen. Rupertus, but the 1st Marines had given more than any commander could reasonably expect of even the toughest fighting force. In six days and nights, under the most punishing conditions imaginable, the regiment had suffered 1,838 casualties. That afternoon they were replaced in the line by elements of the 7th Regiment.

'Since dawn the enemy has been concentrating their forces, vainly trying to approach Higashiyama [Walt Ridge], and Kansokuyama [Hill 300], with 14 tanks and one infantry battalion under powerful aid from air and artillery fire. However, they were again put to rout, receiving heavy losses' – for once the Japanese report did not exaggerate.

Further to the west, the 2nd Battalion of the 7th Regiment, scaling almost sheer cliffs under heavy fire, succeeded in reaching the top of Hill 260 facing the Five Sisters from the west, across a gap which was appropriately to be christened 'Death Valley' (see Map 8, page 143).

On 21 September – D+6 – the III Corps commander Gen. Geiger intervened. When he visited Puller's CP he found the colonel stripped to the waist and with his leg so badly swollen that he could not walk; a fragment of shrapnel that he had picked up during the fighting on Guadalcanal had turned septic and would later require an emergency operation. Geiger drew Puller to one side, and a conversation that witnesses described as 'heated' took place; no one knows what was said, but one of Geiger's staff said much later that it was after this talk that Geiger came to the conclusion that Puller was 'out of touch with reality'.

From there the Corps commander went to Rupertus' HQ and asked to see the latest casualty reports for the 1st Regiment. His worst fears were confirmed: since D-Day the 1st had suffered the heaviest losses by any regiment in Marine Corps history. Ray Davis' 1st Battalion had taken 71 per cent casualties, Russell Honsowetz's 2nd Battalion 56 per cent, and Stephen Sabol's 3rd, 55 per cent.

Roy Geiger told Rupertus that he was going to bring in Army reinforcements. At this point the divisional commander became highly agitated, and said that he could secure Peleliu in another day or two without the help of the Army. Geiger was adamant, however, and instructed that the remains of the 1st Marines be withdrawn to the Purple Beach area to await return to Pavuvu as soon as practicable.

At 6.25pm an urgent message was sent to Gen. Mueller's 81st Division HQ on Angaur to supply a Regimental Combat Team, and within the hour the 321st Infantry under Col. Robert Dark were making ready. On the following morning they began loading, and the next day – D+7 – they were ashore on Orange Beach and heading for the Umurbrogol.

The 1st Marines left Peleliu on 2 October in two hospital ships, and during the voyage 'Chesty' Puller underwent an operation to remove the shrapnel from his leg. He did not know it, but Peleliu was to be the end of the war for this great fighting leader. After recuperating on Pavuvu he returned to America for well-earned and long-overdue leave, and before it was over the atomic bombs had been dropped on Hiroshima and Nagasaki. Lewis Puller went on to distinguish himself again during the Korean War: in the terrible winter withdrawal from the Chosin Reservoir he would again lead his beloved 1st Regiment, in the 1st Marine Division then commanded by Oliver P.Smith. When 'Chesty' finally retired from the Marine Corps in 1955 as a lieutenant-general he was the most decorated Marine in the history of the Corps, with an unprecedented five Navy Crosses.

* * *

The relief of the 1st Marines and the arrival of the Army's 321st RCT signalled a new phase in the battle. Despite the terrible losses incurred during the D-Day landings, Capt. Hunt's battle at the Point, and the 5th Regiment's murderous advance across the airfield, it was gradually becoming apparent that the worst was still to come. The Japanese holed up in the caves of the Umurbrogol were going to have to be levered out individually by the Marines and GIs using point-blank artillery, flame-throwers, bazookas, demolition charges, hand grenades and rifles. The Japanese defenders were doomed; but in this kind of short-range fighting the location of every one of their positions would only be announced by its first burst of fire into the cautiously advancing American infantry exposed on the searing rocks. Victory promised to be costly indeed.

CHAPTER 11

Tightening the Noose

The relief of the 1st Marine Regiment by the 321st RTC took place smoothly; Col. Dark was briefed by Gen. Geiger aboard the *Mount McKinley,* and the regiment came ashore on the Orange Beaches around noon on 23 September. The only remaining element of Puller's regiment, the 3rd Battalion, was relieved by the 2/321st, with the 3/321st in support and the 1/321st in reserve. Dark's first decision was to have the regimental HQ moved further to the rear; he believed that Puller's former location was dangerously close to the front line, and saw no point in endangering his HQ staff needlessly. What the first few days of the battle for the Umurbrogol had proved beyond doubt was that direct frontal attacks against well-prepared enemy strongpoints brought only devastating casualties. There was to be no quick solution.

Colonel Nakagawa had no doubts over how he was going to conduct his defence: he had always intended that every cave, gun position, and strongpoint should be defended to the death, and that their loss would be reflected in equally heavy Marine casualties. On Babelthuap to the north, Gen. Inoue was holding on to his large garrison in the belief that an invasion of the northern island was still a distinct possibility; nevertheless, he decided to send Nakagawa some reinforcements, despite the fact that the colonel had not requested any. On the night of 22 September the first heavy rains since the start of the battle provided Inoue with his opportunity: Maj. Yoshio Iida's 2nd Battalion of the 15th Infantry Regiment set sail across the 20 miles from Babelthuap to the northern shores of Peleliu.

Claims and counterclaims abound about the success of this operation. The US Navy say that they intercepted seven barges when the destroyer USS *H.L.Edwards* located them off Akarakora Point; one was reported sunk and the others were attacked the following morning by naval vessels, aircraft and shore-based artillery. In the early hours of 24 September another landing attempt was made; this time the *H.L.Edwards* claimed 14 barges sunk, and at dawn aircraft and artillery blasted the survivors.

Japanese reports made no mention of these losses, merely stating that elements of the 2/15th Infantry made successful landings on 22 September, and that nine barges arrived safely on Peleliu on the 24th. What is certain is that US intelligence sources later confirmed that between 300 and 600 men of the 2/15th Infantry were now fighting on Peleliu – evidence that a considerable proportion of Inoue's reinforcements did indeed survive to join Nakagawa's command. To secure the area, US amphibious patrols were rapidly deployed and air search missions became a regular feature. A narrative of the 3rd Armored Amphibian Tractor Battalion states:

'On the night of September 22nd, D+7, the Japanese had sent several barges full of fresh infantry to Peleliu from the main base at Koror; on D+9 and D+10, 3rd Battalion units were rushed to the north end of the island to dispose of the remaining barges and to make sure that no further reinforcement occurred. It was during this barge interdiction effort that newsreel cameramen caught Lt. Mike Mihalic with his crew finishing off Japanese survivors from the September 22nd convoy.'

What had become obvious to both the Marines and the Army was that the north of Peleliu and the adjoining Ngesebus Island would soon have to be occupied, not only to prevent any further influx of reinforcements but to isolate and surround the Umurbrogol.

* * *

'There were actually two Pelelius after the first two weeks of the battle', Gen. Oliver Smith was to observe years later. 'One was the flat ground we had captured on the southern third of the island – there [, all but unmolested,] we went about the job we'd been sent to do: seize the airfield and bring in our men and planes so that the Japanese couldn't use the island to interfere with MacArthur's operations in the Philippines. The other Peleliu began at Bloody Nose Ridge and extended northward through the Umurbrogol to Ngesebus Island; this was a brutally different extra-innings ball game, one where the score was kept in the number of ridges taken and how many Marines were killed or wounded in the seemingly endless process.'

In later life, Gen. Smith was to confide to close friends that 'he often wondered why we didn't simply leave the highlands to the Japanese, keep bombing and shelling them from offshore and from the parts of Peleliu we held until there were too few left to continue to fight'.

The encirclement of the Umurbrogol got off to a good start on 23 September – D+8. The 2nd Battalion of the 321st RCT sent patrols northward up the West Road towards the village of Garekoru (see Map 7, page 129). Keeping to the left side of the road in a largely wooded area, they came under sporadic fire from enemy emplacements on the ridge system at the foot of the Umurbrogol, and approached Garekoru (or what little was left of it after days of naval bombardment) by late afternoon. Upon learning that they were almost at Garekoru, Rupertus directed the Wildcats to advance as far as they could before nightfall.

A little after 5.00pm the 2/321st moved on, but soon ran out of cover and into open ground where they came under heavy enemy fire from the ridges to their right. Colonel Dark decided that with night approaching he would dig in and resume the attack the following morning.

The bad weather cleared and 24 September – D+9 – dawned bright and sunny. At 6.00am the Navy began a concentrated bombardment of the western Umurbrogol followed by air attacks on the ridges; no sooner had the planes disappeared than Marine and Army artillery took up the

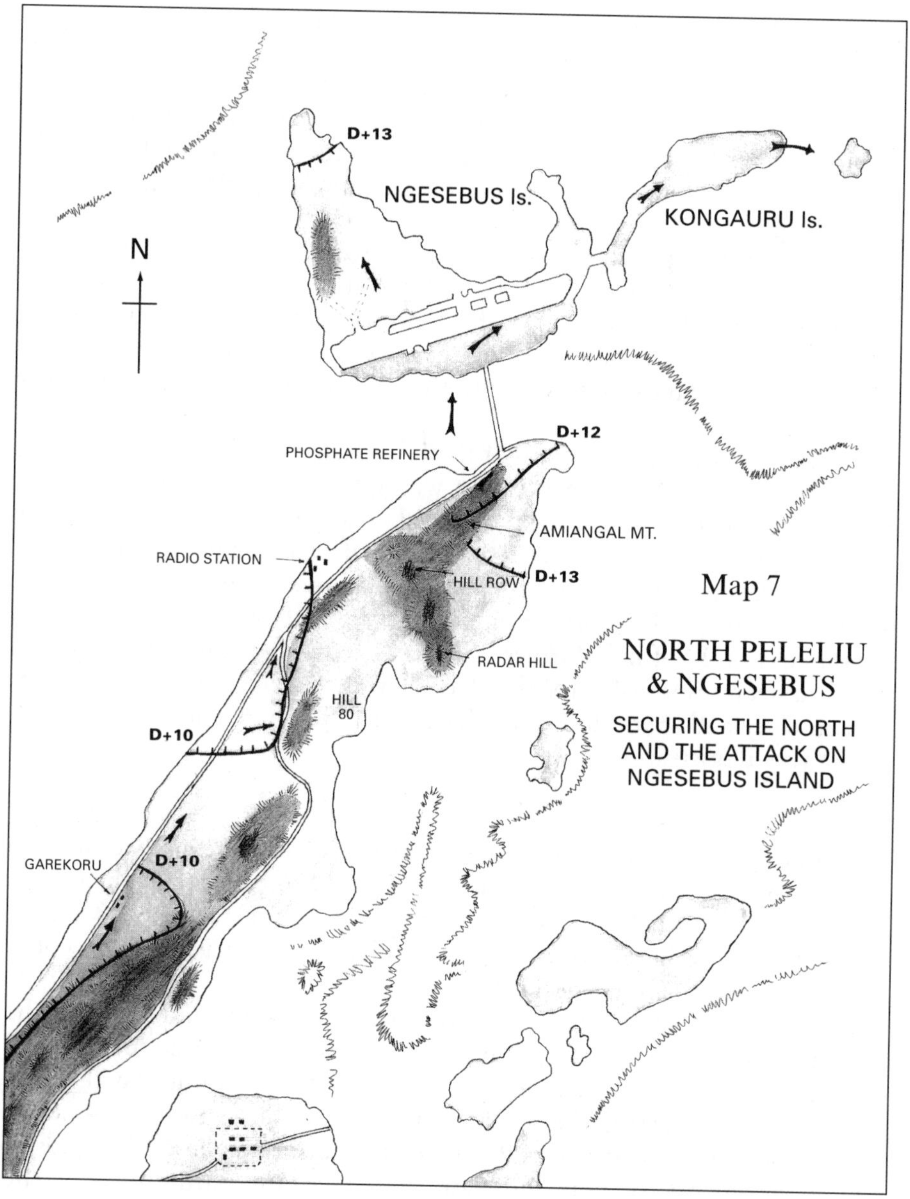
D+13
NGESEBUS Is.
KONGAURU Is.
N
D+12
PHOSPHATE REFINERY
AMIANGAL MT.
RADIO STATION
HILL ROW
D+13
Map 7
RADAR HILL
NORTH PELELIU
& NGESEBUS
HILL
80
SECURING THE NORTH
AND THE ATTACK ON
NGESEBUS ISLAND
D+10
GAREKORU
D+10

barrage, homing in on the Japanese defensive positions north of Garekoru. The 2/321st Infantry jumped off at 7.00am, and around noon discovered a trail which passed through a swamp and disappeared into the Umurbrogol. Leaving Company E to investigate, Dark's GIs moved onward against moderate opposition and secured the ruins of what had been Garekoru. At 4.00pm the Wildcats halted just north of the village and established a defensive perimeter while tanks and a flamethrower unit went forward to reconnoitre. After advancing for over a mile they turned back, having taken note of a number of enemy strongpoints on the ridges to their right.

To protect his right flank as he advanced towards Garekoru, Dark had despatched elements of his 2nd and 3rd Battalions to patrol the ridge system in the foothills along the right-hand side of the West Road. At some stage these troops came under what they described as 'fairly heavy Japanese fire' and moved down on to the road, thus leaving the right flank exposed.

Fortunately the 3rd Battalion of the 7th Marines under Maj. Hurst had been bringing up Dark's rear. Hurst was aghast when he saw the troops scrambling down the hillside and on to the road; he realised that the enemy were in a position to swarm down and cut off Dark's advanced units. He was left with no alternative but to send his Marines to plug the gap and, in what was to be the heaviest fighting of the day, secured the Army's flank for the loss of 27 of his Marines killed and wounded. The Army captain who had been responsible for this débâcle was relieved of the command of his company and spent the remainder of his time on Peleliu working with the Graves Registration Unit.

* * *

The discovery of the trail that led eastwards from the West Road into the Umurbrogol some 300 yards south of Garekoru potentially had huge implications. Did it lead clear across the hills to the East Road? Was it negotiable? If so, here was the point at which Nakagawa's garrison could be cut off from the north and isolated.

The GIs of 'Easy' Company moved across the swamp and followed the trail up into the hills; although narrow in places, they realised that it could be improved and widened. Soon, however, they encountered the first serious obstacle barring their way: a knoll (later named Hill 100 – not to be confused with the other Hill 100 at the southern end of Walt Ridge), which reared up to their right and had a commanding view of the surrounding area. The Wildcats moved swiftly to occupy the knoll before the enemy could realise that they were being encircled, and in a bitter struggle gained the summit before nightfall. It proved to be an uneasy night; Japanese infiltrators attempted to cross over from nearby Hill B, east of their position, but were beaten back with substantial casualties.

Next morning, a patrol of Wildcats stormed down the eastern slopes against heavy fire from dug-in enemy positions and reached the East Road by 10.30am. Although the line was tenuous, the bulk of the Japanese garrison on Peleliu was now contained in what was to become known as 'The Pocket' – the capture of the trail (later dubbed the '321st Trail' or 'Wildcat Trail') was a significant development that isolated Col. Nakagawa in his rocky fortress.

* * *

On 25 September – D+10 – Gen. Rupertus transferred the 5th Marine Regiment from the east of the island. Their task was to secure the area west of the uplands known as Kamilianlul Mountain (see Map 2, page 51) and the East Road. The Army's 321st RCT would reinforce the Wildcat Trail and the ground to the east of the 5th Marines. Lieutenant-Colonel Lewis Walt, executive officer of the 5th, was in charge of the Marine operations in this area as Col. 'Bucky' Harris was still indisposed by the injuries sustained on D-Day; Walt established his command post and kept in touch with Harris, who remained in the rear. Simultaneously, the 1st and 3rd Battalions of the 7th Marines were assigned to support the 321st in their northern drive.

The advance went well; infantry, tanks and the LVT-4 'Ronson' flamethrowers moved up the West Road and rapidly overran the positions that had been pinpointed the previous day, and at 3.30pm the vanguard of the 5th Marines passed through Garekoru village. Following behind the 321st and the Marines, the Army 306th Engineer Battalion began clearing debris, filling shellholes and grading and surfacing what had now become the main artery to the north of the island. The flatter terrain enabled tanks and flamethrower LVTs to support the infantry to the full, and by dusk elements of the 5th Marines reached the Japanese radio station 600 yards north of Garekoru. Not wishing to overextend his lines, Col. Harris broke off contact with the 321st and set up his own defensive perimeter.

That night the 1/5th, who were on the edge of the radio station, took the brunt of the enemy's reaction. Some 300 yards to their north two 70mm guns situated on high ground pounded the Marine lines, and artillery and mortars from nearby Ngesebus Island added harassing fire. Japanese infantry mounted a series of counter-attacks throughout the night, all of which were beaten back – indeed, at one stage the Marines made their own infiltration, destroying two machine gun positions.

A note found by the Marines pinned to the body of a dead Japanese soldier caused them a great deal of amusement: 'American brave soldiers, we think you much pitied since landing on this isle despite your pitiful battle. We are sorry that we can give you only fire, not even good water, we soon will attack your army, you have done brave by your duty, now, abandon your guns and come in Japanese military with white flag (or handkerchief), so we will be glad to see you and welcome you as comfortably as we can.' This kind offer was declined by the Marines.

At 6.00am the following morning – 26 September, D+11 – the 3rd Battalion of the 5th Marine Regiment attacked directly to their front against a coral ridge called Hill 80, overran it, pushed on through a swampy area at the rear, and reached the east coast (see Map 7, page 129). While the 2/5th secured the right flank, the 1/5th moved northward towards the Phosphate Refinery at the northern end of the island, but encountered very stiff resistance. To the right of the West Road at the northern limits of Peleliu lay an L-shaped group of hills called the Amiangal Mountains. The southern part of the L comprised four hills named by the Marines Hills 1, 2, 3 and Radar Hill – this was the highest and most easterly of the four, and the site of a radar installation.

Unknown to the Marines, the Amiangals contained the most intricate and complex system of caves on Peleliu, and even the use of tanks and flamethrowers was to have little impact against the multiple layers of passages and galleries. At Hill 1, the 1/5th Marines spent the day pounding away with Shermans and LVT flamethrowers but got nowhere. However, at Hill 2 the battalion's Company B had better luck; the position succumbed by 2.00pm, giving the Marines a flanking advantage against Hill 1. While these battles were raging, the 2/5th, who had remained uncommitted on the right flank, by-passed Hill 1 and advanced northward in the direction of the phosphate plant. Almost at once they came under fire from enemy positions in the Amiangal and from artillery on Ngesebus Island. By nightfall the battalion commander, Maj. Gayle, brought the advance to a halt and set up his perimeter defences.

* * *

Along the Wildcat Trail, the 2nd Battalion of the 321st renewed their assault on Hill B at 7.00am from the west, while the 3/321st attempted to break through from the south and south-west. All went well until the 3rd Battalion came under murderous fire from fortified Japanese positions built into what later became known as 'Wattie' and 'Baldy' Ridges. Clearly, a new strategy was needed. A group consisting of 45 infantrymen, seven tanks – six LVT(A)s and an LVT flamethrower – under the command of Capt. George Neal, the 2/321st's operations officer, was hastily assembled to attempt an encirclement of the hill from the north.

Dubbed 'Neal Task Force', this small but heavily armed battle group started out from near Garekoru at around 10.00am and moved up the West Road until they reached the junction with the East Road; then they doubled back down the East Road until they reached the rear of Hill B – the only opposition that they had encountered on their way was a group of around 15 suicidal enemy soldiers who were rapidly disposed of.

At 4.00pm white phosphorous smoke shells were fired on to the slopes of Hill B, causing a considerable amount of confusion among the defenders. As the 2nd and 3rd Battalions of the 321st RCT attacked from the south and east, the 'Neal' force stormed up it from the north in a three-pronged assault that cleared the Japanese from the hill by 4.45pm. The defenders, as usual, fought to the death, although the Army were able to capture a few Korean labourers. The northern limit of the Umurbrogol was now defined; Col. Nakagawa was surrounded.

* * *

As the sun climbed in the sky and the heat struck through the Marines' sweat-soaked dungarees, a flag-raising ceremony was performed in front of Gen. Rupertus' command post in a shell-pocked concrete building at the northern end of the airfield. Rupertus, Roy Geiger and Oliver Smith, flanked by the three regimental commanders – Puller, Harris and Hanneken – declared Peleliu 'secure' as artillery fire thundered in the hills to the north. The day was 27 September – D+12 – and the ceremony marked the official transfer of overall command from Vice Adm. Wilkinson to Rear Adm. George Fort. If anyone in the rear echelons had a feeling that the battle was approaching its end, this conviction was not shared by the Marines and soldiers clawing their way through the furnace of rocks and coral further north.

* * *

Since the occupation of the airfield the Seabees and Marine Engineers had worked frantically, often under heavy fire, to clear the wreckage and debris and level the ground. Now 4,000 feet of the north-east to south-west runway was operational, and on 24 September the Marines' own flyers had begun to arrive. Admiral Nimitz's headquarters at Pearl Harbor listed the Marine Air Base Peleliu as operational on 26 September, and a squadron of 24 F4U Corsair fighter-bombers under the command of Maj. Robert 'Cowboy' Stout were landed from the aircraft carrier USS *Lexington* 50 miles offshore. Two days later 24 F6F Hellcats, under Maj. John Fitting, flew in from the USS *Wasp*, and operations by this 2nd Marine Air Wing began immediately.

Throughout the remaining weeks of the battle the Marine pilots flew close support strikes against enemy positions throughout the island, often only a few hundred yards ahead of the Marine and Army front lines, and dropped bombs and napalm canisters throughout the gullies and ridges of the Umurbrogol. These missions were among the shortest ever recorded – a Corsair would lift off from the airfield and might drop its bombs or napalm within 15 seconds of take-off. Most pilots didn't even bother to retract their undercarriages; they made a tight turn, and were back on the runway and taking on more bombs within a few minutes.

Spotter planes had been operational even before the Corsairs and Hellcats arrived, and supplied invaluable information for the American artillery. The spotters were small, fragile, slow, and very vulnerable – as was proved when one was shot down by small arms fire near Hill 100 just off the Wildcat Trail. The plane crash-landed behind enemy lines, but the injured crew were rescued by an Army patrol before the Japanese could locate them. What would have happened if the enemy had got there first does not bear thinking about; the torture and mutilation of prisoners was commonplace among Japanese troops in the Pacific.

* * *

Back in the north, the 5th Marine Regiment was continuing its assault on the dug-in positions in the Amiangal 'Mountains'. Here the Japanese 214th Naval Construction Battalion, largely manned by former miners and mining engineers, had constructed what was probably the most invulnerable warren of sub-surface defences in the entire Pacific theatre. With multiple entrances and exits and sited on more than one level, the enemy were seemingly able to appear and disappear at will. Marines would seal an entrance with a demolition charge and call it secure, only to be attacked by the troops that they had supposedly buried, firing at them from somewhere hundreds of yards away.

Major Gayle and his 2nd Battalion had been halted on 27 September at a large anti-tank ditch which had been built to protect the Phosphate Refinery. With heavy fire coming from the now-ruined plant and from the caves in the high ground to his right, he desperately needed armoured support to spearhead his advance. While a Sherman tank-dozer – the only one left of the three that had come ashore with the 1st Tank Battalion – laboured under heavy fire to fill the ditch, Company E patrols pushed into the high ground on the right flank and occupied the crest of the hill. All the while, the Japanese were pouring heavy and very accurate mortar fire into the midst of the 2/5th Marines; Maj. Gayle was seeing men killed all around him, and the situation was becoming critical.

By 8.30am the ditch was filled sufficiently to allow Shermans to cross, and an LVT flamethrower moved forward and thoroughly doused the

Phosphate Refinery, killing over 60 of the enemy and enabling the advance to continue. Harassed by heavy fire from the hills to their right, from artillery on Ngesebus Island to their left, and from a complex of pillboxes and bunkers to their front, the 2nd Battalion battled onwards until noon, when everything ground to a halt – the Marines now encountered the most elaborate cave system on the whole island, which had at one time housed over 1,000 Japanese troops. The official history describes it:

'This extraordinary example of the mining engineer's art occupied the entire nose of Peleliu's northernmost ridge. Its seaward tip loomed directly above the road, here so cramped between the hill and the shoreline as to be barely wide enough for the passage of a single tank, and dominated completely by the cave mouth which faced in this direction. The first tank to attempt getting around the nose was promptly hit, and though it was not knocked out, indications were that a worse fate might await any others so rash as to attempt the passage until some remedial steps could be taken.'

Colonel 'Bucky' Harris devised an ingenious plan for the deployment of his firepower to resolve the problem. While the 11th Marine Artillery laid down a barrage on Ngesebus Island, the Navy pounded Kongauru, the linked island directly to the east of Ngesebus. In the meantime nine Shermans moved along the shore and blanketed the beaches of Ngesebus with smoke shells.

With the offshore island effectively blinded, five LVT(A)-4s mounting short 75mm howitzers churned out on to the reef about 300 yards north of the ridge, and from this seaward vantage point blasted the mouth of the cave. This allowed tanks and an LVT flamethrower to get forward; the 'Ronson' hosed the cave entrance, and the 2/5th Marines were able to consolidate the area and dig in for the night. As one man in each foxhole tried to get a little sleep, they were blissfully ignorant of the full extent of these cave workings – which would remain partially occupied by the enemy for months to come.

* * *

The operation to secure Ngesebus Island was one of the highlights of the whole Peleliu campaign.

Lying some 330 yards off the northern coast, the island was the site of an airfield with a short fighter strip which had been listed as a prime target during the planning of Operation Stalemate. As the battle developed it had become clear that a more important priority was the silencing of enemy guns installed there, and the prevention of further infiltration from Gen. Inoue's garrison on the more northerly islands.

Ngesebus was 2,500 yards long and had been connected to Peleliu by a wooden causeway, now partially destroyed. A reef, over which the water was estimated at about 4 feet deep, now had to be crossed by the attacking Marines.

The plan of attack was drawn up largely by Col. Harris and Lt.Col. Walt and implemented by the 3rd Battalion of the 5th Marines under Maj. John Gustafson. The 'intrepid mermen' of Underwater Demolition Team No.7 had braved Japanese mortar and rifle fire the previous day to carry out a detailed examination of the channel and pinpoint the most suitable crossing places and the shallowest waters.

The attack got under way at 9.00am on 28 September – D+13 – as the battleship *Mississippi* and the cruisers *Denver* and *Columbus* plastered the island for 40 minutes with their heavy guns. As soon as the barrage lifted, Corsair fighter-bombers of 'Cowboy' Stout's VMF-114 roared in at almost tree-top height; they caused such mayhem that a Japanese officer who was later taken prisoner declared that his men had been so terrified that they had had no chance to defend the beach. (The attack on Ngesebus was the first time a Marine landing had been supported entirely by Marine aviation.)

Anticipating a spectacular display, Gen. Rupertus had invited along a party of 'brass', including Rear Adm. Jesse Oldendorf, to witness the show. The official history records that senior officers from the various elements, including the transports, command ships and fire support vessels, were invited to view the attack from a vantage point that provided safety and even a certain amount of comfort. Had they known, one can easily imagine the reaction of the assaulting Marine riflemen who were to provide the entertainment, to this rather 19th-century decision on their divisional commander's part.

The 3rd Armored Amphibian Tractor Battalion had been told the previous day to furnish 30 Amtanks to support the landing. They quickly informed division that they didn't have 30, and calls went out all over the island for units to return to base camp all available vehicles. The camp hummed that night as tractors were repaired and loaded with ammunition; eventually 35 Amtanks were available for the next morning.

The primary role in leading the assault fell to Company A. An LVT(A)-1 of Lt. Boudreaux's platoon led a column of 13 Shermans across a channel between Peleliu and Ngesebus on the right flank of the assault force; the operational plan called for Company K of the 3/5th Marines to lead the infantry attack on the left, Company L on the right, with Company I in reserve. The first three Shermans got swamped because of inadequate waterproofing, but the remainder hauled up onto Ngesebus beach six minutes later. By 9.30am all units were ashore and storming the Japanese strongpoints; 50 of the enemy were killed or captured among the pillboxes that lined the beaches before they could fire a shot.

'Moving slowly, inching our way over the razor-sharp coral and through the thick underbrush, we came to a clearing', recalls Sterling Mace, a BAR man with Company K. 'The squad crouched, hugging the sandy soil, and took up a position along its edge. The unit's lead scout pointed in the direction of a coloured fabric hanging from a nearby shrub. After scanning the area Pfc Thomas "Nippo" Baxter decided to investigate the mysterious cloth – halfway into the open field he abruptly stopped, raised his rifle and fired one round into the brush.

'He signalled towards me with his index finger; as I crept forward he fired again, this time he signalled with two fingers held high. When I got to Baxter I realised that he had come across a sinkhole; I circled around and climbed to the cave entrance. There, no more than fifteen feet below me, were three Japanese soldiers – two were in the prone stance taking aim at Baxter, the third was standing at their feet, looking in all directions as if he sensed my presence. Our eyes made contact; instantly I brought my weapon up and over the rim, opening fire into the cave. The noise of the barrage ricocheted within the cave – when the smoke cleared and the dust settled, all three lay dead.

'Still unsure that there may be more of them inside, I tossed in several hand grenades; further to ensure the enemy wasn't in the rear of the cave a bazooka man sent in a [rocket]; this was followed by a flamethrower spewing its deadly fire through the opening. As we were leaving the secured area we could hear the demolition unit sealing the cave entrance with dynamite.'

There were about 550 Japanese defenders on Ngesebus, but the relatively flat terrain was not in their favour. The best defensive position was a hilly area on the western coast slightly north of the end of the fighter runway. Company L, supported by armour, moved to the right parallel to the airfield and secured the eastern sector, including the adjacent island of Kongauru. Company K moved northwards and attacked the high ground in the west; and by afternoon all but the northern extremity was in American hands – this too would fall the following day, when Shermans destroyed two large-calibre artillery pieces. By mid-afternoon on 29 September the island was declared secure, and elements of the 2/321st came across to relieve Gustafson's Marines and mop up the few remaining stragglers.

Sterling Mace had a scary experience in the late afternoon of the 28th, when he thought that he and his companion had been abandoned in an advanced position: 'Our group leader, [Cpl.] Richard van Trump, ordered me to move forward and take up a position 20 yards in front of the line. I was a BAR rifleman and had to have an assistant to carry the heavy tins of ammunition. Private Charles Allman and I headed into the bush north of our troops; we found a well-camouflaged trough and set up our gear. Throughout the long day we could hear the rattle of canteens and the whisperings of the troops coming from behind us. Then, towards late afternoon, a sudden silence surrounded Charlie and I, an eerie quiet with the only sound being of the crunching of twigs underfoot and the swish of branches being swept aside, but no familiar noise coming from behind.

'I signalled Charlie that something was wrong and we were pulling back. Crawling towards the clearing we found a bloodied and tattered poncho, alongside were 30–40 rounds of unfired cartridges from a Thompson machine gun – the very weapon that our group leader carried. It was at this time . . . with nobody around that we knew that we were in over our heads. Taking a path slowly back to the beach, Charlie and I were furious over the fact of being left behind; before long we were in a sprint, stumbling and tripping, getting entangled in vines and brush along the trail.

'We finally broke out on to the beach and saw our corporal being carried away on a stretcher; his face was a mass of bloody tissue, the lower portion of his jaw was missing as well as his upper cheek. What had happened was that the Japanese had used his code call and he went in their direction only to be ambushed – so when the troops were ordered to pull back Van Trump was unable to tell anybody about us being up in front of the lines. Charlie and I stood as the stretcher went by and we saw a look of relief come across Van Trump's face – our anger subsided.'

Reports say that the 3rd Battalion of the 5th Regiment lost 'only' 40 Marines (15 dead and 25 wounded); Gen. Rupertus was later to talk of 'light', 'slight' and 'meagre' opposition in his reports on the action. In reality what happened on Ngesebus was a textbook example of good planning and execution: an under-strength battalion of Marines, brilliantly supported by concentrated naval gunfire and outstanding air support, defeated an enemy force of around 500 (most of them infantrymen from an elite Kwangtung Army division who had been in action since 1935), killing 440 and capturing 23, all in the space of a couple of days.

As the sun neared the horizon on 29 September the remainder of Gustafson's battalion boarded Higgins boats and were transported to the Purple Beach area, where the remains of 'Chesty' Puller's 1st Regiment were still waiting for transport to take them to Pavuvu.

The original objective had been to secure Ngesebus for its fighter airstrip, but the Marine flyers were to be disappointed – it turned out that the runway was built on a foundation of soft sand and was totally useless.

On 30 September – D+15 – Gen. Rupertus declared that 'organized resistance had ended on Ngesebus Island and all of northern Peleliu has been secured'. Sadly, no one had informed the Japanese defending Radar Hill and the neighbouring strongpoints of this fact.

* * *

On that same day the other battalions of Col. Harris' 5th Regiment began the final stage of their assault on the remaining Japanese defences in the north.

The 1st Battalion mounted its attack on Hill 3 against stubborn resistance, with tanks and bazooka teams spearheading the infantry. An attempt by the Japanese to reinforce the area was broken up by mortar fire, and by 4.00pm the position had been secured. The way was now open for the Marines to concentrate on the isolated Radar Hill, a single dominating 200-foot feature that lay some 2,000 yards south of Peleliu's most northerly tip, Akarakoro Point.

Lieutenant-Colonel Robert Boyd had less than 500 men left in his battalion and the prospect of assaulting this formidable citadel was not something that he relished. Boyd mounted his attack from two sides with his flamethrowers, bazookas and demolition men sealing dozens of the multitude of cave entrances. By late afternoon patrols had reached the summit, but hordes of Japanese troops were still active in the labyrinth of tunnels inside the hill.

Some 500 yards to the north, Maj. Gayle's 2nd Battalion were busy attacking the enemy still holding out in the blackened remains of the Phosphate Refinery and in the caves in the ridges to its rear. Shermans blasted cave mouths with their 75mm guns, but the enemy continued to harass the Marines, and at one point Gayle's men began take heavy fire from their rear from positions near the northern tip of the peninsula which had been 'secured' the previous day. A platoon from Company E was detailed to the area; the enemy were forced out on to the adjoining reef, where they were decimated by Amtanks.

Both Boyd and Gayle wanted to wait until the following day to resume their attacks, but Col. Harris decided that the situation warranted a new approach. A massive 155mm 'Long Tom' gun was brought up to the front and was employed in an entirely novel way. (The gun and its crew were from Maj. George Hanna's 8th 155mm Gun Battalion, which had been set up on the beach in the face of heavy small arms and machine gun fire that killed two of the crew and wounded three others before the position could be sandbagged.) The 'Long Tom', with a range of over 10 miles, was now to be used at such close quarters that the crews had to take cover to avoid being hit by debris from their own shells. The gun methodically worked over cave mouths on Radar Hill, the Phosphate Refinery and the ridges to the rear; at one point its shells exploded an ammunition store on Radar Hill, and huge clouds of smoke billowed out of the main cave mouth. Enemy troops were soon scurrying out of cave openings: 'We could see our machine guns turning these poor guys into mincemeat', said one eyewitness.

During the three-day period 28–30 September, the 5th Regiment had eliminated a total of 1,172 of the enemy – a formidable tally for an area that was supposedly secure. That afternoon a convoy of trucks and Amtracs arrived from the south and the 1/5th and 2/5th Marines were moved to the rest area near Ngardololok to join their comrades of the 3rd Battalion. With the south and the north now firmly in American hands, Col. Nakagawa's men were isolated in a final pocket of caves and fortifications in the Umurbrogol – the location that he had selected and prepared for a last stand long before the first American had set foot on Peleliu.

CHAPTER 12

To the Bitter End

Two full weeks into the operation, with the Japanese comprehensively outnumbered by the Marines and Army, it seemed that the end could only be a formality. But though holed up in an area only 1,000 yards long by 500 yards wide, Col. Nakagawa had chosen, improved, provisioned and equipped the site of his final battle with consummate skill. To the Americans it was a confusing labyrinth, threatening ambush from every corner and crest; to the survivors of the Japanese 14th Division it was a defensive fighter's dream. Nakagawa and his men knew every inch of the Pocket, and their only concern was to use that knowledge to take as many as possible with them when they died.

Colonel 'Hard Head' Hanneken's 7th Marines were ordered to start the final push; the 5th Regiment were still recuperating in the Ngardololok area after completing the Ngesebus operation, and Gen. Rupertus was still resisting the involvement of further Army units. It was around this time that the general ordered the 1st Tank Battalion – down to about a dozen Shermans – shipped back to Pavuvu with Puller's 1st Regiment. Oliver Smith called this 'a bad mistake, and the tanks were sorely missed when heavy mobile firepower was so important'. The armoured role was now entrusted to the Army's 710th Tank Battalion, a full-strength outfit but one whose only combat experience had been the relatively easy two-day action on Angaur.

As if to provide a fitting overture for what was about to unfold, a three-day typhoon hit the Palaus. The landing of supplies and ammunition was out of the question, and shortages developed at an alarming rate. The situation was bad enough for Roy Geiger to radio Guam: 'We need supplies of all kinds, and we need them now.' Within hours transport planes were braving the storm to land tons of ammunition and food.

At first the rain and cooler weather were welcome; the temperature dropped from 110° to around 80°, and the rock-hard earth softened. But the relief was short-lived: the dust soon turned to mud, and weapons were jammed and clogged by a fine mixture of coral and water.

* * *

The southern end of the Pocket, christened Bloody Nose Ridge by the Marines early in the battle, overlooked the airfield and landing beaches; it was here that Puller's 1st Regiment had expended itself in a series of heroic assaults.

A valley known as the 'Horseshoe' (see Map 8, page 143) offered the only practicable route into the Pocket from the south for both troops and armour. At its northern end was the long, narrow 'Fresh Water Pond'. On the right of the valley was 'Walt Ridge', on whose southernmost hill Capt. Pope and his men had made their gallant assault. On the

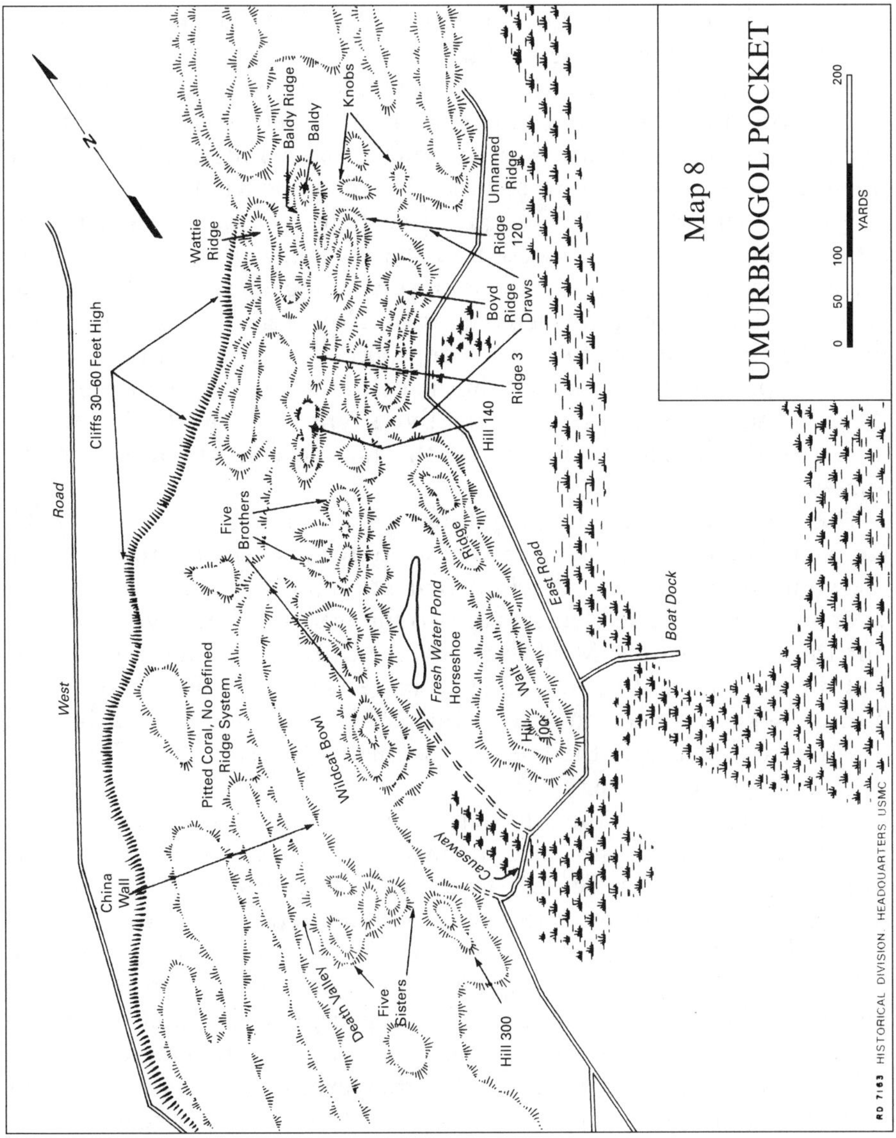
Map 8
UMURBROGOL POCKET
0 50 100 200
YARDS
West Road
Cliffs 30–60 Feet High
Wattie Ridge
Baldy Ridge
Baldy
Knobs
Unnamed Ridge
Ridge 120
Boyd Ridge
Draws
Ridge 3
Hill 140
Five Brothers
Fresh Water Pond
Horseshoe
Ridge
East Road
Boat Dock
Walt
Hill 100
Pitted Coral, No Defined Ridge System
Wildcat Bowl
China Wall
Death Valley
Five Sisters
Hill 300
Causeway
RD 7163 HISTORICAL DIVISION, HEADQUARTERS USMC

left of the Horseshoe was a line of formidable hills named the 'Five Brothers'.

The northern end of the Horseshoe was dominated by three major elevations: from west to east, Hill 140, Ridge 3 and 'Boyd Ridge' (named after Lt.Col. Bob Boyd, who had earlier led a failed attempt to overrun it with the 1st Battalion of the 5th Marines).

North of the Horseshoe, the northern limits of the Pocket consisted of a series of sheer ridges and knobs, all heavily defended: the most formidable were named 'Wattie Ridge', 'Baldy', 'Baldy Ridge', Ridge 120, and three 90-foot-high elevations collectively called 'the Knobs'.

With the 2nd Marine Air Wing in place, fighter-bombers began to play a significant role in the reduction of the Pocket. Flying ultra-low-level sorties from dawn to dark, they bombed and napalmed the whole of the enemy enclave where and when requested. However, although the attacks lifted the morale of the American troops, for the enemy deeply hidden in their complex of caves and redoubts many of these strikes were more of a diversion than a threat; perhaps the flyers' greatest contribution was to defoliate the hillsides and expose the Japanese strongpoints to the attackers.

The next phase of the battle got under way on 30 September – D+15. Colonel Hanneken was hard pressed to stretch his depleted force around the whole of the Pocket, and reinforcements in the shape of the regimental weapons company and elements of two Pioneer companies were brought into the line as infantry. Major Buckley, the CO of the weapons company, had his own method of obtaining 'volunteers': the numerous souvenir-hunters who were found wandering in his area were seized, handed weapons and placed in the line – these men were listed as AWOL until Buckley chose to release them.

The 1st Battalion of the 7th Marines were to move southward on the East Road and attack the adjacent ridges, with part of the 3rd Battalion assisting on their right. By 10.25am the 1/7th had seized one high ridge to the west of the road, but the assault was delayed because of torrential rain and low fog. It was not until afternoon that conditions improved sufficiently for the battalion, supported by tanks and a mortar barrage, to move a further 300 yards south, and failing visibility brought operations to a halt for the day. In probing to the west, units of the battalion had come across a formidable hill, Baldy, and as they explored the base they came under heavy mortar fire and were forced to withdraw. Baldy again resisted the Marines' assault on 1 October – D+16. After struggling for 75 yards in howling winds and driving rain, Company L of the 3/7th came under shredding machine gun fire and the attack petered out.

* * *

Although their fighting strength had been badly eroded (the 3rd Battalion was below 50 per cent and the 2nd below 30 per cent), the 7th Regiment were now ordered to seize Walt Ridge and Boyd Ridge. By consolidating these two important features Gen. Rupertus hoped that he would have a springboard from which the 7th could press westwards while the 5th Regiment – rested after the Ngesebus assault – could move against the Five Sisters, leaving the weapons company, backed by Shermans, to enter the Horseshoe.

The attack on Walt Ridge began at 7.00am on 2 October after a fierce artillery and mortar barrage. The 2nd Battalion of the 7th Marines followed the same route that Capt. Pope had taken on D+4, northwards up the East Road and then across the causeway through the marsh south of the entrance to the Horseshoe. Lieutenant-Colonel Berger and his men achieved complete surprise, and reached the summit of Hill 100 without incurring any casualties. The Japanese recovered rapidly, however, and blasted the Marines from the Five Brothers on the opposite side of the Horseshoe.

As this struggle was in progress, the 3/7th advanced from the south towards Boyd Ridge, but soon became bogged down under heavy fire. Seeking an alternative route, elements of the battalion moved through the swamps alongside the East Road and attacked the enemy flank. By afternoon most of Boyd Ridge had been taken, and a link-up with the 2nd Battalion was achieved before nightfall.

Slightly to the west of the Horseshoe on the far side of the Five Brothers lay 'Wildcat Bowl', the southern entrance to which was dominated by the Five Sisters and Hill 300. With tanks in support, the 3rd Battalion of the 5th Regiment, now rested and reinforced, attacked the Five Sisters and succeeded in taking most of the area; but an increasing volume of enemy machine gun and small arms fire in the afternoon forced them to pull back to their original positions. Sterling Mace, the BAR man from the 3/5th's Company K, remembers the attack:

'Our orders were to take us to another site called Five Sisters . . . a group of coral hills standing 50 feet high; the assignment was to "mop up" the sector and rid it of any stragglers that held on to their posts. We stumbled across a number of dead Marines, some of them lay on stretchers with their bearers lying dead beside them; we found out that they were from the 1st Regiment and had been ambushed on D-Day – for twenty days they had lain there on the rocky terrain unattended.'

At dusk, Mace and his companions made low fortifications from scrap wood and pieces of corrugated iron – digging holes in the diamond-hard coral was out of the question; and with darkness came the inevitable Japanese infiltrators:

'One group came running through our position. As they sprinted past, tossing hand grenades in every direction, the unit, under cover of our tiny forts, opened fire. It was sheer blackness except for the quick flash of grenades going off, [but] suddenly the sky was lit up with star shells – the bursts cast enough light on the enemy for us to see where they were running. I emptied a full magazine at the running shadowy shapes; I reached down to grab another to reload my weapon, but due to the darkness I mistakenly loaded my BAR with tracer bullets – the first blast turned the end of my barrel into a high powered searchlight. [Tracer was avoided so as not to give away ones own position.] At daybreak we found a soldier lying no more than twenty feet from us; he was nearly cut in two from the barrage of lead I [had] fired towards the sound I heard, [but] he still gripped a grenade in each hand. The body count added up to twelve, each one wearing black "pyjamas" and split-toed canvas shoes.'

As Mace and his companions withdrew, staggering from exhaustion, the Japanese lobbed a final mortar barrage at them; one round took the life of Mace's close friend 'Nippo' Baxter.

* * *

During these engagements Col. Nakagawa, who was in radio contact with Gen. Inoue, reported a bizarre picture of the situation: 'About two infantry battalions attacked our position from the north and south; our garrison units repelled them and they withdrew. In this district about 100 enemy troops infiltrated our front lines secretly but were exterminated during the evening. The enemy are estimated at about five infantry battalions, believed to be Marines with one part of the Australian Army.'

On 3 October – D+18 – the 1st Marine Division lost its highest ranking casualty of the battle: Col. Joseph Hankins, CO of the division's HQ Battalion, who was killed at a point in the West Road known as Dead Man's Curve. Sergeant Thomas Climie of the Army's 321st Regiment was an eyewitness to the incident:

'I was told to get my detail of men and load a 2½-ton truck with supplies for the front. We did this, and crawled into the back of an empty truck and our convoy moved up the West Road. We were just getting settled when all hell let loose; bullets were flying everywhere, our sideboards on the truck were being splintered, and the whole convoy was forced to stop. A Jap had a hole chiselled in a rock and his machine gun controlled that whole area of the road. The tailgate of the truck was up so we decided we would go over the sideboards one at a time. I went last, and when the one ahead of me went, just as his hand let go of the sideboard, bullets crashed into where his hand had been. I waited a second or two and then I flew over the side. We all tried to get behind the big tyres while bullets were flying under and over the truck; eventually we crawled to safety behind big rocks.

'I looked down the road at our convoy – jeeps, three-quarter-ton trucks – nothing was moving, everybody had taken cover. Then to my amazement, down the centre of the road came this man striding and cursing and telling everybody to get out and get the convoy moving. As he got near me, about two to three yards, I yelled at him to get down – too late – he went down in a hail of bullets. I found out later that he was Marine Corps Colonel Joseph F.Hankins.

'While we were waiting for a tank to come to suppress the enemy fire one of our group yelled to a guy in the forward foxhole, "How are you?" – answer, "OK". Next they yelled, "Do you need anything?" – answer, "Send some toilet paper".'

* * *

The morning of 5 October – D+20 – saw the 3rd Battalion of the 7th Regiment under Maj. Hunter Hurst (now reduced to less than half of its D-Day strength) commence the assault on Baldy Ridge, a 200-foot-high barrier in the northern sector of the Pocket.

The only approach was guarded by the Knobs, three dome-like hills of about 100 feet elevation which bristled with bunkers, caves and pillboxes. For Hurst's worn-out Marines the task looked daunting; but to their amazement the Knobs were taken with little difficulty. Major Hurst decided to press his advantage and assault Ridge 120, slightly to the south, as a launching point for Baldy hill.

A full-strength 48-man platoon, under 2nd Lt. Dunn, moved forward along a walled ravine, up on to the base of the ridge, and began climbing up among the crevices and rocks with Baldy looming high above. Suddenly a Marine fell to the ground, a bullet through his head, and from the crags all around them a hail of machine gun and rifle fire tore into the hapless platoon. With infinite patience the Japanese had held their fire until the Marines were well up the sides of the ridge, and they now had them ambushed.

The only escape route appeared to be a steep drop from the eastern precipice, and Lt. Dunn lowered himself over in an attempt to lead his men out. Riddled by enemy fire, the lieutenant fell to his death on the rocks many feet below. Three Corpsmen with the platoon did what they could for the wounded, but evacuation looked to be impossible; wounded men were hit again and again. Other Marines attempted to follow Dunn's route, but were either riddled by machine gun fire or fell, suffering broken bones or deep wounds among the sharp coral below. Captain James Shanley, CO of Company L, watching in horror from below, shouted 'Smoke up that hill!', and smoke from rifle grenades slowly wafted around the stricken Marines.

Some jumped, preferring broken bones to certain death where they were. Ten men were left on the ridge – six wounded, a Corpsman who was treating them, and three Marines who stood guard. The wounded told the others to jump: 'You've done all you can for us, now get the hell out of here!', said one. As the thin cover of a cloud of smoke passed across the ridge, the able-bodied men took what they considered to be the only course of action that would give the wounded a remote chance of survival: they rolled them bodily over the edge of the ledge. Anything was better than letting them fall into Japanese hands alive and helpless.

Five dropped like rag dolls, but the sixth got his feet caught in a bush and hung upside down for a time until someone kicked him free. Captain Shanley watched as the crawling survivors struggled through a hail of gunfire towards his lines. Unable to contain himself, he dashed out and scooped up one of the wounded Marines and carried him back; as he ran back to collect another man, a mortar bomb exploded a few feet away and the shards riddled his body.

Shanley's executive officer, Lt. Collis, ran out into the smoke to help him but was immediately shot dead at his side. Two other Marines who had survived the drop from the ledge also ran out to help their comrades, but died before they could reach them. Captain Shanley was evacuated, but died before nightfall. Of the 48 men who had climbed the ridge only 11 were alive, and six of those were wounded.

The Baldy Ridge assault was to be the final combat for the 7th Regiment. According to Gen. Oliver Smith, 'Purely and simply, there were no longer enough men left in the outfit to continue the fight'. Even Gen. Rupertus had to concede that they were finished: of the 3,217 who had landed on D-Day, 1,486 were dead or wounded – losses of more than 46 per cent. The 7th Marines were moved out from their scattered positions and driven by the Army to Ngarmoked Island in the south; soon they were sailing back to the dubious comforts of Pavuvu.

* * *

Not quite all of the 7th Regiment escaped the horrors of the Umurbrogol immediately, however – Sgt. James Moll of the 1st Battalion's Company A recalls that his platoon were taken back into the hellhole:

'I think that it was a day or two after we got back to the rest area that a lieutenant came to me and said I was going to take the men in my platoon up into the hills again to see if we could clear out a group of Japs in a pocket. I couldn't believe this, because in the condition we were in I didn't think we were a match for a couple of Boy Scouts. Anyway, we all got our combat gear on again, boarded a truck and off we went. All the time I was on Peleliu I never saw a map, but we were on the west coast just north of where I believe the 1st Regiment landed; they unloaded us on the south end of this high ridge that ran parallel to the beach. The lieutenant pointed towards the hill and said, "They're up there, go get'em", [and] found a position where he could watch our progress with some binoculars.

'We went up the south slope because the others were too steep, I can't remember how high it was but in our condition it felt as though we were climbing the Alps. The footing was bad and it took a hell of a time to get there – when we reached the top I could see the lieutenant watching so I waved to him.

'At the top there was a track going upwards at a slight angle, the width was maybe eight to ten feet. As we moved up the slope 50 yards or so we came upon pits in the ground about three or four feet in diameter and fifteen to twenty feet deep. There must have been at least a dozen of these pits, and in every pit there were maybe five or six dead Marines, one on top of another – they must have been there since D-Day.

'About another 50 yards up the road there was a steeper slope and a vertical wall on the island side and a vertical drop on the coast side. When I got about three-quarters of the way over the pits, the Japs opened fire with a machine gun. All we could do was hang on and lean into the pits as much as possible, we couldn't see the bastards and had no way of firing back – it was a miracle that none of us were hit at this time.

'I could see no way of advancing without getting killed so I told the men to turn around, we were going to try to find another approach. They didn't fire anymore when they saw us turn round, I believe they were short of ammunition – if they had fired mortars at us we would probably have joined the dead. I think those pits were cisterns for collecting rainwater off the higher ridges and what I called the road was a channel to guide the water down the slopes.

'The lieutenant was pretty pissed off when we got back down the hill, but he sort of cooled off when I told him what the conditions were up there. I also told him that if he wanted to go back we would follow him to the end, and said that he should have given us more info about what was up there. He admitted that he didn't know what was up there and was very surprised to hear of all the dead Marines – for all we know those brave Marines may still be in those pits.'

* * *

The only Marine regiment now operational on Peleliu was Col. Harris's 5th. The colonel's attitude is best summed up in his own words: 'The 5th, after careful air and ground reconnaissance, reversed the direction of all prior attacks and made the main drive down from the north.' On 6 October – D+21 – Lt.Col. Bob Boyd's 1st Battalion took over a front which included Walt and Boyd Ridges parallel to the East Road. Major Gordon Gayle's 2nd Battalion stood before Baldy and its supporting mass of ridges and knolls; the 3rd Battalion had been temporarily withdrawn to a bivouac area.

The western perimeter – the 'containing line' – was manned by an assortment of support troops. Towards the north Maj. Harold Richmond, executive officer of the 1/5th, had a group consisting mainly of Pioneers, and to his right Lt.Col. Richard Evans had the 'infantillery' – gunners from the 11th Regiment who had been pressed into service as infantry, plus a mixture of volunteers from other outfits including many from the Amphibious Tractor Battalions.

The weather had improved and the soggy ground was drying out; unfortunately the temperature began to soar, and the Marines found themselves fighting once more in stifling heat. Sanitary conditions on the island were appalling: bodies that had been exposed for days or weeks had blackened and bloated until they ruptured, giving off a revolting stench; piles of faeces lay uncovered, adding to the stink; and huge blowflies were everywhere, feeding on the dead and the filth before coming to cluster around the men's messtins. Dysentery was widespread and almost everyone seemed to be suffering from diarrhoea. Mosquitoes swarmed in dense clouds – luckily they were not the malarial species, but they produced bites that rapidly developed into large irritating lumps. The recently introduced insecticide DDT was widely used; eventually it was sprayed all over the island, particularly in the large areas of swampland, from low-flying aircraft. Private first class Tim Nelson recalls: 'When those planes came over trailing clouds of white dust the shooting suddenly died down – even the Japs let them fly over without shooting at them.'

* * *

Colonel Harris launched a two-pronged attack on the Umurbrogol Pocket on 7 October – D+22. Major Gayle's 2/5th Marines were ordered to continue the assault on Baldy and its ridges from the north, while in the south the 3rd Battalion were to probe the Horseshoe, Walt Ridge and the Five Brothers.

Under intense fire from Baldy, two of the previously evacuated Knobs were recaptured, allowing bulldozers to begin cutting tracks to enable tanks and LVT flamethrowers to move forward in support. In an attempt to expose more of the Japanese fortifications, Corsairs of the 2nd MAW mounted a series of napalm attacks to defoliate the dense woodland.

It was said admiringly of 'Bucky' Harris that he liked to be lavish with his artillery and stingy with the lives of his men. This became evident in the ridges west of the East Road, where he laid on such a devastating barrage that many vertical walls were reduced to steep inclines. Rupertus continued to press his last regimental commander for an early end to the fighting in the Pocket; and Harris, 'with considerable reluctance', ordered a frontal assault on Baldy. This took men of his 2nd Battalion's Company G to the summit; but they could not be reinforced sufficiently to hold it against the inevitable night counter-attacks, and had to back down again at the end of the day. Machine-gunner Jim Johnston recalls:

'On one occasion we fought inch by inch through that ragged terrain and came across the bodies of a bunch of 7th Marines, blackened and swollen, the flies and the birds and the maggots were working on them. It looked to be what was left of a platoon of good, young Marine Corps riflemen and machine gunners – it was repulsive beyond imagination.'

On the same day the Shermans of the Army's 710th Tank Battalion ventured into the Horseshoe following a two-hour-long artillery barrage. The Shermans rumbled in from the East Road and reached the Fresh Water Pond, blasting enemy caves in the sides of Walt Ridge and the Five Brothers on either flank as they went. Encouraged, they replenished their fuel and ammunition and returned for a second attack at 12.15pm supported by LVT flamethrowers and 1st Engineer Battalion demolition and mine-lifting teams. Heavy fire rained down on the intruders as the tanks pounded the cliff walls, killing many of the enemy, but as soon as their ammunition ran low the Shermans were forced to make a hasty retreat. Once they were deprived of their armoured support the situation became untenable for the infantry.

While this attack was in progress in the Horseshoe, over to the left Company L of the 2/5th Marines passed into Wildcat Bowl, parallel and slightly to the west, which was bounded on one side by the western slopes of the Five Brothers and on the other by a ridge later to be christened the 'China Wall'. The Japanese reaction here was the most vicious that the Marines had yet encountered; unknown to them, they had ventured to within 200 yards of Col. Nakagawa's headquarters in a deep cave embedded in the north-west end of the bowl.

* * *

Major Gayle's assault in the north characterised the slow, grinding advance that was to become the norm in the Umurbrogol. Bulldozers painstakingly cleared paths for the advance of the LVT flamethrowers (whose narrow and vulnerable tracks were not made for rocky terrain). The 'Ronsons' then systematically burned off the dense vegetation shrouding the enemy positions. Infantry bazooka teams blasted caves, while patrols probed for alternative access routes at the rear of the Baldy complex. These efforts continued for the next few days; Harris's tactics placed a higher priority on thoroughness than on speed, despite the constant pressure from divisional headquarters. Gordon Gayle said of his Marines: 'Every man fighting in those hills is an expert – if he wasn't, he wouldn't be alive.'

On 9 October – D+24 – a patrol from the 2/5th's Company G reached the summit of a ridge to the west of Baldy and established an enclave there; the position connected with Baldy Ridge and provided direct access to Baldy itself. It was promptly named 'Wattie Ridge' after the platoon leader, Lt. Robert Wattie. The morning of 10 October saw Wattie, now supported by Army howitzers, making a direct assault across Baldy Ridge. The enemy mounted strong opposition, but the Marines kept up the momentum and by noon the ridge and Baldy itself were in American hands. The capture of Baldy allowed Company E to launch an assault from the east that afternoon, and by evening on D+25 the full length of Ridge 120 had been secured.

Piling on the pressure, the 2nd Battalion resumed their southwards drive towards what had been chosen as their final objective – Hill 140, a dominating position just north of the Five Brothers. Jim Johnston was involved in these operations early in October:

'We moved south down the East Road and got in position to make another assault in the hills; we paused to rest for a few minutes, [and] as I started to sit down I heard a strange sound, like a *whirr*. I looked up and saw a blinding flash of light; the world spun, and then it was very dark. From somewhere in the distance I heard people ask, "What's his serial number?". Slowly consciousness ebbed back into my brain and I opened my eyes – the world was still dark gray.'

Johnston had been hit in the head by a piece of shrapnel; his wounds were attended to, and he was able to make his way back to the little tent that passed as a hospital. While there he saw a Marine with a bad stomach wound, who asked for a cigarette, and smoke came out of the wound below his rib cage. 'I said to the doctor, "Sir, I think somebody should look after this boy, he's pretty bad." The doctor's eyes lowered and he said, "I'm sorry, son, he's dead – he just doesn't realise it yet."'

Company G pressed on southwards along Baldy Ridge until they reached the ravine that separated them from Hill 140; meanwhile, Company E attacked on a parallel course on their left, along the slopes of Ridge 3. Company G moved down from the ridge and the forward elements of both units made a frontal attack on Hill 140 supported by Company F, who had been brought forward from reserve. These attacks by the 2nd Battalion of the 5th caught the Japanese napping, and Hill 140 was secured by 3.00pm that day; the rest of the afternoon was spent in mopping up overrun positions. The battalion – miraculously – had suffered only two men killed and ten wounded in return for one of the most important positions in the Pocket.

Realising the significance of their failure to hold the feature, the Japanese mounted a night counter-attack on Hill 140 but were repulsed with heavy losses. This achievement was to mark the end of the 2/5th Marines' participation in the battle for Peleliu. Early the next day, 12 October – D+27 – the exhausted Marines were relieved by the 3rd Battalion. Major Gayle's men drifted down from the hills for a desperately needed rest before their eventual return to Pavuvu. Jim Johnston's comment sums up the feelings of one of the survivors:

'As we sailed away I watched until the battle-blackened ridges and peaks of Peleliu were out of sight, and silently reaffirmed that I never wanted to see that place again . . . I have heard recently that someone later raised a monument [there] to the boys who fought and died on Peleliu – I think that was a bad idea. If I were going to put up a monument, I would put it on the lawn of the White House in Washington DC.'

* * *

On 12 October, 28 days into the battle, Adm. George Fort declared the 'Assault Phase' of Operation Stalemate to be over, and ordered the replacement of the 1st Marine Division by the Army's 81st Division. For Gen. Roy Geiger the announcement came as a blessed relief.

The III Amphibious Corps' commander had long felt that the Marines should be pulled out, but knew that to do so he would have to either relieve Gen. Rupertus of his command or directly order him to withdraw his remaining units from the Umurbrogol. The former course of action would have meant the end of Rupertus' career, and even the latter would seriously jeopardise his future in the Corps. Now Adm. Fort had saved Geiger from a painful decision.

Within two days, Col. Dark's 321st Infantry began taking over the Marine positions around Baldy and Hill 140, on the slopes of the Five Brothers and the Five Sisters and near the China Wall. Colonel Venable's 322nd RCT was ordered from Angaur to garrison southern Peleliu and the Ngarmoked Island area.

The remaining 5th Marines took over the area previously occupied by the 81st on Ngesebus Island and near the ruined Phosphate Refinery – an area now boasting the luxury of tents, showers and a cookhouse.

The men rested and ate, cleaned themselves up, and waited for the transport *Sea Runner* to take them back to the Russell Islands. Jim Johnston again:

'We went back to Pavuvu, back to the same company areas and squad tents we had left when we headed for Peleliu. [There were] empty spaces all over the place – at least we didn't have to build a dry place to sleep again. As much of a shithouse as Pavuvu was, it was heaven compared to where we had been, it almost felt like home. It may seem odd but several men who had made it through Peleliu committed suicide after we got back to Pavuvu. I feel bad when I think of the guys who gave up on the world and killed themselves there – I don't blame them and I can understand it, but it still makes me feel bad.'

On 30 October, Gen. Geiger officially handed over the command of Peleliu to Gen. Mueller and his 81st Division. The 'three days' predicted by Gen. Rupertus had developed into 46 days, with still no end in sight; 1,121 Marines had been killed and 5,142 wounded – and the enemy still held the heart of the Umurbrogol Pocket. Generals Geiger and Rupertus flew out at 2.00pm for Guadalcanal; Gen. Oliver Smith stayed on to liaise with Mueller during the transition.

* * *

So far the 81st Division's role in Operation Stalemate had been limited to the invasion of Angaur by the 321st and 322nd Regiments, and to acting as support to the Marines in the northern push towards Ngesebus Island. Now the full weight of defeating the Japanese in the Umurbrogol Pocket would fall upon their shoulders.

In the meantime the 321st Infantry had tied up some minor loose ends. To the north of Peleliu lay a string of small islands stretching northwards towards Eil Malk Island; there was a possibility that some were occupied, and Mueller was determined that there would be no more reinforcement of Nakagawa's garrison. On 9 October the 2nd Battalion of the 321st began a series of landings north of Ngesebus to mop up any enemy troops on these islands. On the nearest, Garakayo, the Army encountered some machine gun fire but occupied the island by early afternoon; on nearby Cordoray there was also some slight resistance, but it too was occupied on the same day. On the 10th, the unoccupied islands of Ngemelis, Arimasuku and Garyo were seized; the northern perimeter was now completely secure.

General Mueller made his deployments around the Pocket as follows. The 3rd Battalion of the 321st covered the eastern section – the summits of Walt Ridge, Boyd Ridge and the entrance to the Horseshoe. The 2/321st held the top of Hill 140 with additional positions to the west of the hill.

The 1st Battalion of the 323rd held a line in the south, facing the Five Sisters and Death Valley.

The morning of 16 October saw the battle resume in earnest. The 2nd Battalion of the 321st moved south from Hill 140 in an attempt to capture the first of the Five Brothers, but came under murderous machine gun fire and were forced to retire. To the south the 1/323rd pushed forward on the 17th, but advanced only 100 yards before they had to call off the attack under savage fire from positions on the Five Sisters.

Further attempts by the 2/321st to secure the Five Brothers on 19 October brought a temporary success when Company E reached the top of Brother 1 shortly before noon and the top of Brother 2 a few hours later; but heavy fire from the remaining Brothers and a determined counter-attack forced the exposed Wildcats back to their original positions. The effect on morale of having to give up ground so hard-won, knowing it was all to do again, may easily be imagined.

Seeing the futility of wasting his troops in costly assaults against almost impregnable defences, Gen. Mueller now opted for a policy of 'siege warfare'. Nakagawa's men were contained in an area measuring little more than 800 yards by 400 yards, with no hope of reinforcement and with food, water and ammunition diminishing. With the departure of Gen. Rupertus there was no pressure for a speedy conclusion to the battle. From now until the end, the reduction of the Pocket became a grimly methodical business.

Thorough preparation preceded each assault: large scale artillery and mortar barrages paved the way for all troop movements; bulldozers cleared paths to previously inaccessible enemy strongpoints for tanks and LVT flamethrowers; and the Marine flyers of Maj. Stout's VMF-114 dropped hundreds of napalm canisters from recklessly low altitude – at times these air strikes were made so close to the American lines that unfuzed canisters were dropped and ignited later by tracer fire. The Army engineers displayed a remarkable degree of ingenuity: a 300-yard pipeline was constructed leading from the West Road to supply a long-range flamethrowing system, and floodlights were erected to illuminate the Fresh Water Pool in the Horseshoe – the only remaining water source for the Japanese.

The strength of the surviving enemy garrison was a mystery; estimates of between 500 and 1,200 were made, but shortly after the 81st took over, Col. Nakagawa reported to Gen. Inoue that 'our total garrison units number about 700 soldiers, including the slightly wounded'.

The reduction in the urgency of the infantry advances did not make the fighting any easier for the GIs; as the Japanese lines shrunk, resistance increased proportionally. The Wildcats – fighting their first and only battle of the war – acquitted themselves excellently. Amid the 'undiggable' rocks of the Umurbrogol the humble sandbag became an integral part of infantry tactics. With little or no cover and only concrete-hard coral under foot, the sandbag became the only cover available to troops in the front line. Sand was trucked up from the beaches and rear echelon troops spent hours filling the bags. Once an attack got under way, sandbags became as important as ammunition – the GIs crawled up to blind crests pushing their sandbags ahead of them with long poles.

* * *

General Mueller made the north of the Pocket his priority on 21 and 22 October. The 1st Battalion of the 323rd RCT succeeded in extending its front by 100 yards, while the 2/321st, closely supported by artillery and Marine Corsairs, assaulted and recaptured Brothers 1, 2 and 3 in a two-day battle.

In the east, the 3/321st entered the Horseshoe with tanks and flamethrowers to blast caves along the eastern base of the Five Brothers. The flamethrower – a particularly horrible weapon – proved to be the most effective method of forcing the enemy from the depths of the hundreds of caves that riddled the ridges and walls of the Umurbrogol. Private first class Hank Chamberlain describes a typical attack:

'I was cover for a flamethrower near a row of caves. A grenade came flying out towards us – we dived behind an outcrop of rocks to our left and the grenade exploded harmlessly. As the flamethrower guy stumbled forward, my pal Bucky and I emptied our magazines into the cave entrance . . . to keep the occupants quiet for a while. The flamethrower was now alongside the cave entrance and sidestepped in front of it and let off a long blast. A single Jap came tearing out, he was a mass of fire from head to foot and his shrieks were indescribable. Both Bucky and I had emptied our guns into the cave and we reloaded as fast as we could. The Jap was now writhing on the ground with his arms flailing the air; we put him out of his agony with enough bullets to kill a dozen men.'

The intermittent heavy rain and shrouding fogs which had characterised the weather since the beginning of October continued to play a part in slowing down operations, and it was well into November before there was a significant improvement.

The reduction of the Horseshoe continued and the 323rd RCT, all of whose units had recently returned from Ulithi, now began to take over from Col. Dark's 321st Infantry. By 26 October command in the Pocket had been transferred to the 323rd's Col. Arthur Watson. Taking advantage of the improving weather, Watson mounted renewed assaults in the southern sector; the 2nd Battalion finally took complete control of Hill 300 and the Five Sisters, and the 3/323rd began advancing along the ridgeline of the China Wall flanking Wildcat Bowl.

Unknown to the GIs, they were once again within yards of the cave that housed Col. Nakagawa's and Gen. Murai's headquarters, and the enemy resistance was fearsome.

As the end approached the Japanese increased their night-time incursions into the Army's lines; they were particularly successful on the evening of 17 November, when a sniper killed Lt.Col. Raymond Gates, the CO of the 323rd's 1st Battalion – the highest ranking Army officer to die on Peleliu.

By now, tanks and LVT flamethrowers had unhindered access to Wildcat Bowl and Death Valley. The Five Brothers were finally cleared out by 23 November, and the few remaining Japanese were surrounded in their caves in the China Wall and among the hillocks above Death Valley.

Army engineers constructed a ramp from the floor of Wildcat Bowl to the crest of the China Wall, enabling tanks and flamethrowers to bring the last enemy strongpoints under direct fire. Now confined to an area about 150 yards long, the Japanese were under constant attack from all directions.

Colonel Nakagawa sent a final message to Gen. Inoue on Koror on 24 November, saying that he could not last for more than one more day; he was reduced to 50 able-bodied men with 70 wounded. At 4.00pm on that day – the 71st day of the battle for Peleliu – both Col. Kunio Nakagawa and Maj.Gen. Kenijiro Murai committed suicide. The 81st Division report noted: 'The enemy has fulfilled his determination to fight to the death.'

* * *

Diehard individuals continued to cause casualties among the American forces, and these troglodytes were still being winkled out until the end of the war. In April 1947 a retired Japanese admiral was brought to Peleliu, and persuaded an officer and 26 men to give themselves up to the US forces. In 1949 a Peleliu native was accosted by a Japanese soldier who wanted to surrender. A final survivor surrendered to the locals in 1954, and returned to Japan as a hero.

Like so many of his predictions, Gen. Rupertus' contention that the Army were not up to the job had proved to be wrong. The Army were responsible for almost a quarter of all enemy troops killed on Peleliu, and sustained proportionally fewer casualties. The 1st Marine Division's special action report of 1945 claimed 10,695 of the enemy killed, and the division had 6,786 casualties – 1 Marine for every 1.62 Japanese.

The 81st Division claimed 3,249 of the enemy killed on Peleliu, and suffered 1,290 casualties – 1 soldier for every 2.66 Japanese.

Of course, given the nature of the battlefield these figures are only approximate; and by themselves they tell us nothing about the relative experiences of the two divisions. The overriding fact was that the Army was not part of the initial landing force, nor was it engaged in the heavy fighting of the first week in the Umurbrogol. Even so, they confirm that the Wildcats were involved in fighting that was every bit as savage and demanding as that of the Marines. For troops who had never been in combat before the Angaur–Peleliu operation, their performance cannot be faulted.

CHAPTER 13

The Reckoning

Although Peleliu was one of the major battles of the Pacific War, equalling Tarawa, Iwo Jima and Okinawa in its sheer savagery, it has languished in obscurity for over 55 years – an unknown battle fought on an island abounding in unpronounceable names, and eclipsed by events elsewhere in the Pacific and Europe. The distinguished writer William Manchester – himself a Marine sergeant, severely wounded on Okinawa – describes it as being 'hidden away like a guilty secret'. Question marks still hang over certain aspects of the planning and leadership of the operation; and looming behind them all is the question – should the battle have been fought at all?

Operation Stalemate 1 was planned to neutralise the considerable Japanese presence in the Palau Islands prior to Gen. MacArthur's intended invasion of Mindanao in the southern Philippines. The island of Yap, the anchorage of Ulithi and the Palau islands of Babelthuap, Peleliu and Angaur were all earmarked for invasion in a large-scale operation that would involve three divisions – two Army and one Marine. But the early occupation of Saipan, Guam and Tinian, the major islands of the Marianas, and the virtual destruction of the Japanese naval and air presence in the battle of the Philippine Sea, rendered the Palaus relatively unimportant. A considerably scaled-down plan – Stalemate 2 – restricted the Palaus operations to the 1st Marine Division assault on Peleliu and the Army's occupation of Angaur, with elements of the 81st Division available as reinforcement if necessary.

Admiral Marc Mitscher's Operation Desecrate 1 at the end of March had destroyed all Japanese shipping and most aircraft on Peleliu. The enemy had no physical means of transporting their troops from the Palaus to the Philippines, and the overwhelming superiority of the US Navy's dozens of carriers, battleships and cruisers sealed off the Palau Islands from the outside world before the first Marine stepped on to the beach. Admiral Halsey's recommendation that MacArthur should shift his invasion further north in view of the negligible Japanese presence in the Mindanao area – a view accepted by the Joint Chiefs of Staff and MacArthur himself – was the final confirmation that the Palau garrison posed no serious threat to MacArthur's flank.

Yet Adm. Nimitz, while agreeing with these general proposals, did not include any change to the Stalemate 2 plan in his recommendations. The reason why must remain obscure, though there is some evidence to suggest that he considered the Palaus an important springboard in a much larger scheme, also favoured by MacArthur, to move north from the Philippines into Formosa and China, from where they would mount the final assault on the Japanese mainland. If this was a decisive factor in Nimitz's decision, then Peleliu is an example of a huge sacrifice of lives in the interests of an operation that never took place. Hindsight, however, makes us all faultless strategists; to second-guess a commander of the calibre of Chester Nimitz half a century after the event is not an excercise which should be lightly undertaken by armchair generals.

* * *

Shortcomings in the organisation and direction of the battle are easier to identify.

From Tarawa onwards the planning of all the major Marine assaults had been entrusted to three brilliant commanders: Vice Adm. Kelly Turner, a master of the organisation of amphibious operations; Rear Adm. Raymond Spruance, Nimitz's right-hand man and chief strategist; and Lt.Gen. Holland Smith, the irascible Marine commander. During the planning of Operation Stalemate 2 the 'big three' were almost totally occupied with the assault on the Marianas, and their expertise would be sorely missed. We may recall the description by a 1st Marine Division staff officer of communications between Pearl Harbor and Pavuvu during the preparatory phase as being like jungle drums.

The list of errors and omissions was long. The choice of Pavuvu for the recuperation of an exhausted division and its training for the invasion was appalling. The planners did not allow for the limitations of aerial photo reconnaissance of Peleliu, particularly of the Umurbrogol uplands, and the invasion maps gave no indication of the true nature of the terrain. During the embarkation for Peleliu ships failed to arrive on time, with the result that a third of the Sherman tanks had to be left behind.

The greatest enigma of all was Gen. Rupertus – his moody, uncommunicative and unimaginative personality cast a shadow over the whole operation. His six-week absence in Washington during the vital planning stage was astonishing. Yet though he left his second-in-command Oliver Smith to do the bulk of the detailed preparatory work, Rupertus thereafter not only treated him with a marked lack of respect, but actively excluded him from command decisions.

It would be a harsh critic who condemned Rupertus for not reporting his accidental injury shortly before the operation; but given that his hampered mobility ensured that he would not be on the beach himself during the opening stage of the landings, his outright order to his subordinate commanders that they were to disregard any change to the original instructions which might be ordered by Gen. Smith – the senior officer on the spot – is astonishing. As the battle developed and Rupertus' originally predicted three-day timetable was revealed as fantasy, the general's reluctance to accept Army troops to reinforce Puller's shattered 1st Marines was probably damaging, and certainly contributed to the steady deterioration of the relationship between Rupertus and his Corps commander Gen. Geiger.

At one stage during the battle, Col. 'Bucky' Harris of the 5th Marines called at Divisional HQ to find Rupertus in tears. 'Harris, I'm at the end of my rope', he said; 'two of my fine regiments are in ruins. You usually seem to know what to do and get it done – I'm going to turn over to you everything we have left. This is strictly between us.' Obviously, Rupertus could not have taken such an action without ending his career on the spot; but his outburst clearly reveals his mental state as the battle became too much for him.

Rupertus had been seen by many in the Marine Corps as Gen. Alexander Vandegrift's protégé; some even considered that he was being groomed as his possible successor as Commandant of the Corps. That all changed after Peleliu. Soon after he arrived back on Guadalcanal with Geiger he was summoned to Washington where he had a private meeting with Vandegrift; nothing is known of what was said, but an aide later reported that the meeting was 'acrimonious'. Rupertus was appointed to command the Marine Training Schools, a position generally recognised as a sideways step which signalled the decline of his career; as compensation he was awarded the Distinguished Service Medal, regarded by some 'Old Breed' officers as totally unwarranted. Rupertus was not to record his own opinions of the battle as did so many others. After attending a dinner party at Washington's Navy Yard in March 1945, he collapsed and died of a massive heart attack on the doorstep of his quarters; he was 55 years old.

* * *

From the end of the battle until the surrender of Japan nine months later, the aircraft of the 2nd Marine Air Wing continued to mount raids against the garrisons on Babelthuap, Koror and the other islands to the north. Heavy enemy anti-aircraft fire claimed the lives of a number of pilots, among them Maj. Robert 'Cowboy' Stout, VMF-114's commanding officer.

The Seabees laboured to repair and extend the Peleliu airfield, and a massive airstrip was hacked out of the scrubland on nearby Angaur. Neither airfield was ever used for their intended purpose – to support

MacArthur's campaign in the Philippines – and the Palaus became a backwater as the war moved north to Iwo Jima and Okinawa.

Although the Angaur and Peleliu airfields were never to be used as major operational bases, one of them was to play a part in saving 316 American lives. On the night of 30 July 1945 a veteran of the Peleliu bombardment force, the cruiser USS *Indianapolis*, was – as is now notorious – sailing alone and under conditions of great secrecy mid-way between Guam in the Marianas and Leyte in the Philippines; she had recently delivered components for the atomic bomb to Tinian, and was now steaming for the US Navy base at Tacloban. A few minutes after midnight three torpedoes from the Japanese submarine I-58 slammed into her side, and she sank in less than 15 minutes; the explosion had put the ship's radio room out of action and no distress signal was transmitted.

On the morning of 2 August a Lockheed Ventura twin-engined patrol aircraft left the airfield on Peleliu and headed north. At 11.00am, almost at the limit of his patrol, the pilot, Lt. Gwinn, spotted a long oil slick, and dropped to 5,000ft to investigate. His crew were amazed to see dozens of men in the water, and immediately summoned help. Soon a PBY Catalina flying boat arrived, followed by the destroyer USS *Cecil J.Doyle*, and by late afternoon seven ships were converging on the scene. Of the 900 sailors who had gone into the water only 316 survived; the remainder had died of wounds, burns, thirst and shark attacks.

* * *

For its conduct on Peleliu the 1st Marine Division was awarded the Presidential Distinguished Unit Citation. General Rupertus was replaced by Maj.Gen. Pedro del Valle. The division remained on Pavuvu – resting, rebuilding itself, and training – for five months. On 15 March 1945 it shipped out for its last invasion of the war: Okinawa in the Ryuku Islands, only some 325 miles south of Japan itself. In scope this was an operation vastly greater than Stalemate 2: Okinawa is a large island some 60 miles long, which was garrisoned by around 80,000 Japanese troops of Gen. Ushijima's 32nd Army plus about 30,000 'home guards'. For the invasion Lt.Gen. Simon Buckner's 10th Army of seven divisions included the 1st, 3rd, 4th and 5th Marine Divisions and Army formations. Admiral Kelly Turner commanded the landing fleet, supported offshore by Adm. Marc Mitscher's carriers of Task Force 58.

The 1st Marine Division landed on 1 April on the west coast between Yontan and Kadena airfields; and in complete contrast to their last landings, these were virtually unopposed. The similarity to Peleliu was to be revealed later: Ushijima had concentrated his best troops in a deep, complex system of fortifications in the south of the island. The Marines and GIs faced a grinding three-month battle in miserable weather to capture Okinawa ridge by ridge, bunker by bunker. By the time Gen. Ushijima committed suicide on 21 June, the 1st Marine Division had suffered 1,115 killed, 6,745 wounded and 41 missing. The division was still on Okinawa when the atomic bombs brought the war against Japan to an end.

In October 1945 the division was shipped out – not home, but to China. For another year the 'raggedy-arse Marines' would hold garrisons in the Tientsin, Tangshan and Chinwangtao region, to 'carry out the provisions of the surrender and maintain law and order' – a mission which brought almost daily 'incidents' with bandits and Communist guerrillas. The division finally returned to the United States in October 1946.

* * *

The outstanding bravery and fighting qualities of both the Marine and Army units involved in the battle for Peleliu have never been in doubt. The Marines stormed the invasion beaches under vicious enemy fire, and fought in conditions and temperatures that were almost unbearable. They advanced across the airfield in exposed formations, and shattered the Japanese tank attack on D-Day. Under constant pressure from the divisional commander, the 1st Regiment virtually expended itself in the early fighting on Bloody Nose Ridge. The 5th and 7th Regiments who relieved the 1st Marines were also bled dry, battling heat, thirst, sheer cliffs and razor-sharp coral under relentless fire from a deeply dug-in enemy who made them pay with lives for every heart-breaking yard. The Marines, and later the GIs of the 81st Division, displayed a level of courage and devotion to duty that transformed what could have been seen as a dubious venture into a battle that should be remembered with awe in America's military annals.

APPENDIX 1

US Marine Corps Command & Staff, Peleliu

(SOURCE: HISTORICAL DIVISION,
HQ US MARINE CORPS, 1950)

EXPEDITIONARY TROOPS

Commanding General	Maj.Gen. Julian C.Smith
Chief of Staff	Col. Dudley S.Brown
F-1	Col. Harry E.Dukelberger
F-2	Lt.Col. Edmund J.Buckley
F-3	Col. Robert O.Bare
F-4	Lt.Col. Jesse S.Cook Jr

7th Anti-Aircraft Artillery Battalion

Commanding Officer	Lt.Col. Henry R.Paige
Executive Officer	Lt.Col. Elmer C.Woods
Bn-3	Capt. Hugh J.Irish

III AMPHIBIOUS CORPS

Commanding General	Maj.Gen. Roy S.Geiger
Chief of Staff	Col. Merwith H.Silverthorn
C-1	Lt.Col. Peter A.McDonald
C-2	Col. William F.Coleman
C-3	Col. Walter A.Wachtler
C-4	Col. Francis B.Loomis Jr

CORPS TROOPS

1st Amphibian Tractor Battalion

Commanding Officer	Maj. Albert F.Reutlinger (to 21 September) Capt. Arthur J.Noonan (from 22 September)
Executive Officer	Capt. Thomas H.Boler (from 23 September)
Bn-3	Lt. Norman H.Bryant

6th Amphibian Tractor Battalion

Commanding Officer	Capt. John I.Fitzgerald Jr
Executive Officer	Lt. Whitley A.Cummings Jr

8th Amphibian Tractor Battalion

Commanding Officer	Lt.Col. Charles B.Nerren
Executive Officer	Maj. Bedford Williams
Bn-3	Lt. John R.Tull

3rd Armored Amphibian Tractor Battalion

Commanding Officer	Lt.Col. Kimber H.Boyer
Executive Officer	Maj. Arthur M.Parker Jr
Bn-3	Lt. Marvin E.Mitchell

12th Anti-Aircraft Artillery Battalion

Commanding Officer	Lt.Col. Merlyn D.Holmes
Executive Officer	Lt.Col. Edwin A.Law (to 18 October)
	Lt.Col. Kenneth A.King (from 19 October)
Bn-3	Maj. Joseph R.Jacyno (to 10 October)
	Capt. Whitman S.Bartley (11–25 October)
	Capt. Henry H.McUmber Jr (from 28 October)

3rd 155mm Howitzer Battalion

Commanding Officer	Lt.Col. Richard A.Evans
Executive Officer	Maj. Lewis A.Jones (to 25 October)
	Maj. Hunter C.Phelan Jr (from 26 October)
Bn-3	Maj. Daniel S.Pregnall

8th 155mm Gun Battalion

Commanding Officer	Maj. George V.Hanna Jr
Executive Officer	Maj. Robert F.Meldrun
Bn-3	Maj. Hunter C.Phelan Jr (to 25 October)

1st MARINE DIVISION

Commanding General	Maj.Gen. William H.Rupertus
Asst. Division Commander	Brig.Gen. Oliver P.Smith
Chief of Staff	Col. John T.Selden
D-1	Maj. William E.Benedict (to 23 September)
	Lt.Col. Harold O.Deakin (from 24 September)

D-2	Lt.Col. John W.Scott Jr
D-3	Lt.Col. Lewis J.Fields
D-4	Lt.Col. Harvey C.Tschirgi

Division Headquarters Battalion

Commanding Officer	Col. Joseph F.Hankins (to 3 October)
	Lt.Col. Austin C.Shofner (from 3 October)

1st Tank Battalion

Commanding Officer	Lt.Col. Arthur J.Stuart
Executive Officer	Maj. Donald J.Robinson
Bn-3	Lt. Ernest A.Hayden Jr

1st Service Battalion

Commanding Officer	Col. John Kaluf
Executive Officer	Maj. Charles F.Rider

1st Motor Transport Battalion

Commanding Officer	Capt. Robert B.McBroom
Executive Officer	Capt. George G.DeBell
Bn-3	Lt. Walter M.Greenspan

1st Pioneer Battalion

Commanding Officer	Lt.Col. Robert G.Ballance
Executive Officer	Maj. Nathaniel Morgenthal
Bn-3	Capt. Warren S.Sivertsen

1st Engineer Battalion

Commanding Officer	Lt.Col. Levi W.Smith Jr
Executive Officer	Maj. Theodore E.Drummond
Bn-3	Maj. Eugene T.Schoenfelder

1st Medical Battalion

Commanding Officer	Cdr. Emil E.Napp, USN

(Regiments:)

1st MARINES

Commanding Officer	Col. Lewis B.Puller
Executive Officer	Lt.Col. Richard P.Ross Jr
R-1	Lt. Frank C.Sheppard
R-2	Capt. James W.Horton

R-3	Maj. Bernard T.Kelly
R-4	Maj. Francis T.Eagan
1st Battalion, 1st Marines	
Commanding Officer	Maj. Raymond G.Davis
Executive Officer	Capt. James M.Rogers
2nd Battalion, 1st Marines	
Commanding Officer	Lt.Col. Russell E.Honsowetz
Executive Officer	Maj. Charles H.Brush Jr
Bn-3	Capt. Robert W.Burnette (to 18 September)
	Lt. Bernard J.Baker (from 19 September)
3rd Battalion, 1st Marines	
Commanding Officer	Lt.Col. Stephen V.Sabol
Executive Officer	Maj. William McNulty
Bn-3	Maj. Jonas M.Platt
5th MARINES	
Commanding Officer	Col. Harold D.Harris
Executive Officer	Lt.Col. Lewis W.Walt
R-1	Capt. Alan F.Dill (to 16 September)
	Capt. Paul H.Douglas (from 16 September)
R-2	Capt. Levi T.Burcham
R-3	Maj. Walter S.McIlhenny (to 16 September)
	Capt. Donald A.Peppard (from 17 September)
R-4	Maj. Joseph S.Skoczylas (to 30 September)
1st Battalion, 5th Marines	
Commanding Officer	Lt.Col. Robert W.Boyd
Executive Officer	Maj. Harold T.A.Richmond
Bn-3	Maj. Hierome L.Opie Jr (to 15 September)
	Capt. Edwin B.Glass (from 16 September)
2nd Battalion, 5th Marines	
Commanding Officer	Maj. Gordon D.Gayle
Executive Officer	Maj. John H.Gustafson (to 15 September)
	Maj. Richard T.Washburn (from 16 September)
Bn-3	Maj. Richard T.Washburn (to 15 September)
	Capt. James H.Flagg (from 16 September)

3rd Battalion, 5th Marines	
Commanding Officer	Lt.Col. Austin C.Shofner (to 15 September)
	Lt.Col. Lewis W.Walt (night 15/16 September)
	Maj. John H.Gustafson (from 16 September)
Executive Officer	Maj. Robert M.Ash (to 15 September)
	Maj. Hierome L.Opie (from 16 September)
Bn-3	Maj. Clyde A.Brooks
7th MARINES	
Commanding Officer	Col. Herman H.Hanneken
Executive Officer	Lt.Col. Norman Hussa
R-1	2nd Lt. Richard F.Spindler
R-2	Capt. Francis T.Farrell
R-3	Maj. Walter Holomon
R-4	Maj. Hector R.Migneault
1st Battalion, 7th Marines	
Commanding Officer	Lt.Col. John J.Gormley
Executive Officer	Maj. Waite W.Worden
Bn-3	Maj. Lloyd W.Martin
2nd Battalion, 7th Marines	
Commanding Officer	Lt.Col. Spencer S.Berger
Executive Officer	Maj. Elbert D.Graves (to 20 September)
	Maj. John F.Weber (from 21 September)
Bn-3	Maj. John F.Weber (to 20 September)
	Capt. Lee W.Langham (from 21 September)
3rd Battalion, 7th Marines	
Commanding Officer	Maj. E.Hunter Hurst
Executive Officer	Maj. Victor H.Streit
Bn-3	Maj. William J.King
11th MARINES (ARTILLERY)	
Commanding Officer	Col. William H.Harrison
Executive Officer	Lt.Col. Edson L.Lyman
R-1	Lt. Robert M.Alderson
R-2	Capt. Richard W.Payne (to 24 September)
	2nd Lt. Ralph W.Smith (from 25 September)

R-3	Lt.Col. Leonard F.Chapman Jr
R-4	Capt. Lewis F.Treleaven

1st Battalion, 11th Marines

Commanding Officer	Lt.Col. Richard W.Wallace
Executive Officer	Maj. James H.Moffatt Jr
Bn-3	Maj. John R.Chaisson

2nd Battalion, 11th Marines

Commanding Officer	Lt.Col. Noah P.Wood Jr
Executive Officer	Maj. Floyd C.Maner (to 15 September)
	Maj. John P.McAlinn (from 16 September)
Bn-3	Capt. David R.Griffin

3rd Battalion, 11th Marines

Commanding Officer	Lt.Col. Charles M.Nees
Executive Officer	Maj. William J.Hannan
Bn-3	Capt. William R.Miller

4th Battalion, 11th Marines

Commanding Officer	Lt.Col. Louis C.Reinberg
Executive Officer	Maj. George E.Bowdoin
Bn-3	Maj. Elliott Wilson

APPENDIX 2

Estimated Japanese Strength, Peleliu

(SOURCE: HISTORICAL DIVISION, HQ US MARINE CORPS, 1950)

IMPERIAL ARMY: *14th DIVISION:* *2nd Infantry Regiment* (incl. 1 artillery battalion)	3,283
3rd Bn/15th Infantry Regiment (incl. artillery company, 4 × 75mm, & mortar company, 10 × 81mm)	1,030
Divisional tank company (less one platoon), 12(?) × Type 95 *Ha-Go*	c.100
Misc. divisional units (signals, intendance, field hospital)	c.300
53rd Independent Mixed Brigade: *346th Independent Infantry Battalion*	685
IMPERIAL NAVY (Combatant): *45th Naval Guard Force* (part)	(?) 200–400
114th & 126th Anti-Aircraft Units	600
IMPERIAL NAVY (Labour): *204th & 214th Naval Construction Battalions,* (parts) *43rd & 235th NC Bns*	(?) 2,000–2,200
IMPERIAL NAVY (Airfield personnel): Peleliu	1,270
Ngesebus	950
Total	**(?) 10,320–10,700**

Select Bibliography

Alexander, Joseph H., *Storm Landings,* Naval Institute Press (Annapolis, Maryland, 1997)

Cameron, Craig M., *American Samurai,* Cambridge University Press (Cambridge, 1994)

Davis, Burke, *Marine: The Life of 'Chesty' Puller,* Little Brown & Co (Boston, 1962)

Davis, Ray, *The Story of Ray Davis,* Research Triangle Publishing (N. Carolina, 1995)

Fane, Francis, *The Naked Warriors,* Appleton Century Crofts Inc (New York, 1956)

Gailey, Harry A., *Peleliu 1944,* Nautical & Aviation Publishing (Annapolis, 1983)

Gilliland, Ann Owens, *Peleliu Remembered,* Booker Publications (Fort Worth, Texas, 1994)

Green, David M., *Peleliu – After the Battle No 78,* Battle of Britain Prints Int (Plaistow, 1992)

Gayle, Gordon D., *Bloody Beaches,* USMC Historical Center (Washington DC, 1996)

Hough, Frank O., *The Assault on Peleliu,* Historical Division USMC (1950) – *referred to in text as 'the official history'*

Hallas, James H., *The Devil's Anvil,* Praeger (Westpoint, Connecticut, 1994)

Johnston, James, *The Long Road of War,* University of Nebraska Press (Lincoln, Nebraska, 1998)

Lindemann, Klaus, *Desecrate 1,* Pacific Press Publications (Belleville, Michigan, 1998)

Lea, Tom, *Battle Stations,* Still Point Press (Dallas, Texas, 1988)

Ross, Bill D., *Peleliu – Tragic Triumph,* Random House (New York, 1991)

Rottman, Gordon, *US Marine Corps 1941–45,* Osprey Publishing (London, 1995)

Watkins, Richard Bruce, *Brothers in Battle,* (private publication)

Waterhouse, Charles, *Marines and Others,* Sea Bag Productions (Edison, New Jersey, 1994)

Woodard, Larry L., *Before The First Wave,* Sunflower University Press (Kansas, 1994)

Zaloga, Steven Z., *Armour of the Pacific War,* Osprey Publishing (London, 1983)

Index